The Li

of

Outrageous Excuses

4471 Pacific Coast Hwy,
apartment a 106

THE LITTLE GIANT® ENCYCLOPEDIA

of Outrageous Excuses

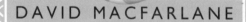

DAVID MACFARLANE

Sterling Publishing Co., Inc.
New York

Compiled by: David Macfarlane

Book Design: Richie Taylor

The author has strived to be as accurate as possible with the exact wording of direct quotes and with the attribution to original sources listed in the book. Our apology in advance for the misrepresentation or inaccuracy due to the reprinting of sources.

Library of Congress Cataloging-in-Publication Data available

10 9 8 7 6 5 4 3 2 1

Published by Sterling Publishing Co., Inc.
387 Park Avenue South, New York, NY 10016
©2006 by David Macfarlane
Distributed in Canada by Sterling Publishing
C/o Canadian Manda Group, 165 Dufferin Street,
Toronto, Ontario, Canada M6K 3H6
Distributed in the United Kingdom by GMC Distribution Services,
Castle Place, 166 High Street, Lewes, East Sussex, England BN7 1XU
Distributed in Australia by Capricorn Link (Australia) Pty. Ltd.
P. O. Box 704, Windsor, NSW 2756, Australia

Printed and Bound in China
All Rights Reserved

Sterling ISBN-13: 978-1-4027-1926-4
        ISBN-10: 1-4027-1926-4

For information about custom editions, special sales, premium and corporate purchases, please contact Sterling Special Sales Department at 800-805-5489 or specialsales@sterlingpub.com.

Contents

The Nature of Excuses

Consider for a moment the fundamental tendencies of the human species. What do we do? What do we all do? Well, for starters, we eat, sleep, drink, laugh, cry, mourn, recreate, procreate, eliminate (as in waste), work, clean (some more than others), observe, and think. We do all these things, more or less compelled by biology so that we may survive and function.

Howbeit, these are not the most interesting behaviors of the human family. The truly savory characteristics are those we develop when we interact with others or participate in a particular culture. Within this realm, behaviors in the context of love, marriage, parenting, work, and sex vary far and wide; and we each create reasons to laugh, cry, procreate, sleep, eat, and mourn. In fact, this connection between relating to one another and assigning reasons to each of our behaviors is key because it gives rise to something else we all do: make excuses. One might even say that making excuses is another biological function, a compelled behavior from which we can extricate ourselves only with the aid of almost superhuman resolve or holy grace.

Think about this for a moment. When was the last time you heard anyone say, "Yes, I did it. It's my fault, and I take full responsibility"? This kind of accountability has become so rare that we look at anyone who would utter such idiotic blasphemy with suspicion: "This guy's clearly up to something. Nobody's stupid enough to just own up to things like that."

To be fair, the overwhelming majority of excuses served up are attempts to avoid responsibility for minor events and conditions: being late for work, uttering an insensitive remark, failing to hand in homework, or violating a traffic regulation. But then there are those behaviors so monstrous, so inexcusable, society stands aghast that anyone would have the unmitigated gall to utter a weak-kneed defense: think of Timothy McVeigh, Ted Bundy, or Richard Nixon. In these more extreme circumstances, society finds itself unable to accept excuses because to do so would be to condone the behavior and make anything and everything open to some sort of rationale. Such is the societal logic of attempting to excuse oneself from personal behavior.

No, it's not a particularly entertaining or amusing direction to take with regard to the subject of this book, but it is both interesting and relevant. Is there a connection between making excuses for being late to work and making them for embezzlement or fraud? For the most part, no, yet the slippery slope that runs from the least to the most egregious excuse includes a component common to all who avoid the mea culpa: a desire to avoid pain. When most individuals realize they might suffer from the choices they've made, they'll do or say just about anything to get out of the mess they're in.

Is it deviant, immoral, or unethical to try to circumvent pain with excuses? Not really, except in extreme cases, but problems can arise here and there if excuse-making becomes pathological or habitual. How does your boss react to you coming in late every day for a month? Probably even the most creative and unique excuses will fail you in this kind of situation. But take heart, excuse-maker; if you can recognize your behavior, you can change it. If you see yourself in this book—and if you're human, you will—you'll become increasingly aware of the excuses you make and you just might make the effort to change. Before you know it, they'll be asking you to head up committees at work. After all, you'll be the only one who doesn't make up excuses for not doing it.

What Is an Excuse?

Okay, when you get right down to it, what is an excuse, really? Well, unless it is the retelling of an event that actually happened, it can be only one thing: a lie. Yes, that's what I said, a lie. Taking this a step further, we might say a rationalization is a lie we tell ourselves, while an excuse is a lie we tell others. Of course, we never think of excuses in this particular way, so let's not do so now. The L-word will not appear again from this point forward.

It is important to differentiate between an excuse and a reason. How are they different? Well, legitimacy is a distinguishing characteristic. For example, when a batter strikes out and says afterward, "I didn't go to the plate with my usual bat," we can accept that as an excuse. After all, he still had the opportunity to swing the bat at the ball, and he missed it anyway. Could a different bat have made a difference? Perhaps, a little, Yet not in any legitimate or acceptable way.

Contrast that with the batter who strikes out and says later, "Boy, that pitcher was throwing heat. I couldn't come near the ball." That is a reason. It is legitimate, truthful, involves both individuals in the equation (the pitcher and the batter), and recognizes that success and failure sometimes occur despite our best and worst efforts.

Now consider the student who simply forgot to do her homework and then says her computer crashed and the document was lost. That is (in absence of the banished L-word) a fib, a canard, a prevarication—and it is an excuse. An excuse that, in certain unlikely situations, might be necessary in order for the student to graduate high school and get into college. So is there an ethical dimension to excuses? Or are they are a sure sign of the moral decline from which our nation irredeemably suffers?

Well, we've hit that moral crap a little hard in recent years, don't you think? Excuses are what they are: common among us all. This book is intended more as entertainment than sermon; it is a weekend trip to the amusement park, not a Sunday afternoon in the chapel. Or should we say, it's mostly the amusement park, with a little chapel thrown in for good measure. That's just the unavoidable nature of excuses—one side of the coin is shiny and fun, and the other is dull and weathered.

A Few (Notorious) Words About Excuses

As you ponder the nature of excuses and the implications of the excuse for human behavior—if pondering is something you like to do—factor in the words of wisdom thinkers throughout history have passed on to us. We hope these words will either help you to take full advantage of the excuse or move you to put it on a shelf, available for only periodic and absolutely necessary use.

"Excuses change nothing, but make everyone feel better."

—*Mason Cooley*

"Any excuse will serve a tyrant."

—*Aesop, 550* B.C.

"One unable to dance blames the unevenness of the floor."

—*Malay proverb*

"He that is good for making excuses is seldom good for anything else."

—*Benjamin Franklin*

"Your letter of excuses has arrived. I receive the letter but do not admit the excuses except in courtesy, as when a man treads on your toes and begs your pardon— the pardon is granted, but the joint aches, especially if there is a corn upon it."

—*Lord Byron*

"We need to hear the excuses men make to themselves for their worthlessness."

—*Margaret Fuller*

"It is not difficult to deceive the first time, for the deceived possesses no antibodies; unvaccinated by suspicion, she overlooks lateness, accepts absurd excuses, permits the flimsiest patchings to repair great rents in the quotidian."

—*John Updike*

"And oftentimes excusing of a fault / Doth make the fault the worse by the excuse."

—*William Shakespeare, King John*

"Difficulty is the excuse history never accepts."

—*Edward R. Murrow*

"A real failure does not need an excuse. It is an end in itself."

—*Gertrude Stein*

"Cynical realism—it's the intelligent man's best excuse for doing nothing in an intolerable situation."

—*Aldous Huxley*

"Temptation is the woman's weapon and the man's excuse."

—*H. L. Mencken*

"Man gives every reason for his conduct save one, every excuse for his crimes save one, every plea for his safety save one; and that one is his cowardice."

—*George Bernard Shaw*

"Two wrongs don't make a right, but they make a good excuse."

—*Thomas Szasz*

"For many people, an excuse is better than an achievement because an achievement, no matter how great, leaves you having to prove yourself again in the future, but an excuse can last for life."

—*Eric Hoffer*

"The trick is not how much pain you feel, but how much joy you feel. Any idiot can feel pain. Life is full of excuses to feel pain, excuses not to live, excuses, excuses, excuses."

—*Erica Jong*

"Sometimes, people use age as a convenient excuse. 'I'm too old to start something new,' or, 'I couldn't learn that at my age.' Other people, though, go on to achieve their greatest accomplishments in life in later years."

—*Catherine Pulsifer*

"An excuse is worse and more terrible than a lie, for an excuse is a lie guarded."

—*Alexander Pope*

"Nothing is impossible; there are ways that lead to everything, and if we had sufficient will we should always have sufficient means. It is often merely for an excuse that we say things are impossible."

—*Francois La Rochefoucauld*

"I attribute my success to this—I never gave or took any excuse."

—*Florence Nightingale*

"We have forty million reasons for failure, but not a single excuse."

—*Rudyard Kipling*

"He who excuses himself, accuses himself."

—*Gabriel Meurier*

"Uncalled-for excuses are practical confessions."

—*Charles Simmons*

Creative Excuse Making: A Four-step Process

1. Choose a person, object, or event external to yourself on which to pin your unacceptable behavior. Always put the blame on something that can't defend itself. Children, pets, inanimate objects, and relatives living in foreign countries make perfect scapegoats. Utilize the designated person, object, or event to construct a sentence in which the offending substance or happening is either the subject or object.

Examples:

Excuse as object: "I ran into a black rhinoceros on my way to work."

Excuse as subject: "My body temperature is below freezing."

2. Think about your audience. What is your relationship with the person to whom you are making an excuse? What kind of excuse is ideal for this person? Is an excuse the right approach for this person?

3. Think about the tone of your excuse. Should you approach this with a slightly nasal whine? Should you appear animated and flustered? Would a confident and direct approach work best? Would something utterly ridiculous work to distract attention from you? Is something blatantly ribald in order? Should you just use

a straightforward and believable excuse? Also, consider whether or not endless blather can be your friend. If you prattle on ad nauseam, will the listener soon lose interest and fail to even hear what you are saying? In the right scenario (talking to a frantic boss), it just might work.

4. Embellish your excuse with realistic-sounding and authoritative words and phrases to lend weight and believability to your excuse. Add the names of pharmaceuticals or diseases (see "The Medical Excuse"), throw in Latin words or phrases, exploit little-known cultural traits and traditions, and recycle obscure facts around which to build an excuse.

Examples:

Cultural

"My parents raised me in an Israeli kibbutz."

"Among the Masai, women do most of the physical work."

"In Japanese culture, the entire group is responsible for failure."

"I'm fasting in recognition of Kwanzaa."

Illnesses/Medical

"I've come down with twenty-four-hour beriberi."

"This Neomycin is really making me woozy today."

"My doctor put me on pills to try and reverse the lobotomy."

"I've never had a worse case of rhinoplasty in my life!"

Latin Words or Phrases

"I was having trouble with my vox populi this morning."

"I had to get my doctor to take a look at my habeus corpus."

"I feel like I'm coming down with amicus curiae."

"My doctor said I have the worst case of pluribus unum he's seen."

Rules to Observe When Making Excuses

The feebleness or banality of an excuse should never be a deterrent to its use.

Certain ailments work better than others as excuses. No doctor or machine in the world can prove that you don't have a headache.

Try to remember that nature allotted each of us only two grandmothers whose funerals we can attend.

Easy Targets

If you lack a person, object, or event within your personal realm of experience on which you can focus your excuse, broaden your search. Here is list of ideal targets for placing blame. And just why are they ideal? Well, they are public, hence well known, but more importantly, they are almost impossible to refute!

The right-wing conspiracy	Big government
Gridlock	A communist plot
Trickle-down economics	The evangelical right

Christopher Columbus	The New World Order
Bill Clinton	Corporate America
George W. Bush	The economic slowdown
Ralph Nader	The IRS, taxes
Ronald Reagan	Unions
Dick Cheney	Mass hysteria
The liberal media	Pork-barrel spending
Right-wing radio	The lying Republicans
Michael Moore	The deceitful Democrats
FOX News	The government shutdown
Saturday-morning cartoons	The rich
The United Nations	The poor

Irrational exuberance

Partisan politics

Catastrophic success

The Swift Boat Veterans

Historical revisionism

Faulty intelligence

Cultural relativism

The French

Voters in Florida

Preservatives

Fluoride

Junk food

NutraSweet

Wheat gluten

Angry white men

Angry black men

MTV

That rap music

El Niño

Hormones

Disorganized government

Welfare mothers

Gay marriage

Organized religion

Declining morals

The devil

Foreigners

The new
millennium

Joe Camel

Asbestos

Self-righteous red states

Degenerate blue states

Ignorant voters

Bad exit polling

Gay marriage

Activist judges

Hanging chads

Rigged voting machines

The politics of fear

Corrupt foreign
governments

Florida

Ohio

The culture of death

Religious absolutism

How to Use This Book

Well, you could use this book to prop open a door, kill flies, press flowers, assault your boyfriend, or stabilize a wobbly table. Better yet, thumb through the pages and amuse yourself, share a few passages with friends, call upon what you've learned when you find yourself in sticky situations, and study the vagaries of human behavior.

If nothing else, this book should give you a wealth of ideas, so that next time you need to blame something you did or did not do on something or someone else, you should not fall short. Before retreating with the truth, you can consider all of the possibilities we've given you here: Could your cat be blamed? The government? The stars? Your upbringing? The idea initially is to give you flexibility, to open your eyes to the wonderful medley of excuses just thriving and teeming all around you. You live in a Petri dish of excuses—the world—and you've likely not seen it yet for all its potential.

Of course there will inevitably be a situation in your life for which you will not find specific excuses herein. In that case, demonstrate just a bit of ingenuity and improvise—replace a few words, rework sentences, revise concepts. We believe this book to be the best source of excuses you'll find, and if you can't find what you need here . . . well, don't blame us.

Quite literally, this volume is intended as an amusing reference source. The first section covers the most common yet effective excuses known to man: the medical excuse, the meteorological (weather-related) excuse, the proverbial excuse, and the nonsensical excuse. The second section organizes excuses by audience. When you find yourself in need of an appropriate excuse for an employer, an educator, an officer, a spouse, or some other special someone, you'll find an excuse here to fit most any occasion. The third section is organized by topic. Whether you're evading a fitness program, nursing an addiction, or plotting an invasion of a foreign country, you're sure to find material you can use in this section. Browse topics as needed or just start here and go page by page. Soon you'll recognize excuses you've heard slip from your own mouth, and you'll begin to truly realize that excuse-making is as common as sucking in oxygen or visiting the facilities.

Excuse-makers: that's who we are. Might as well embrace it!

Later in this book we'll cover excuses tailored to particular audiences and situations. But first, let's lay some groundwork for effective excuse-making by going over the four most flexible and robust types of excuses: the medical excuse, the meteorological excuse, the proverbial excuse, and, of course, the nonsensical excuse.

The Medical Excuse

"I had to get something out of my gastrointestinal system."

Medical excuses work well because most people won't dare seem so insensitive as to doubt that your pain is real. But in order to be convincing, you've got to understand how a good medical excuse works. Medical excuses may rely on sympathy, humor, fear, or bewilderment. If you can't tug at your victim's heartstrings or make him or her laugh, instill in your victims the fear of contagion. If that doesn't work, confuse them with technical and obscure medical terminology. A simplistic excuse might well be enough to appeal to a person's sympathy or humor, but fear and bewilderment take a bit more craft.

Basic Medical Excuses

"I need to check on something that's bleeding."

———•◆•———

"My glass eye fell out and rolled under
the washing machine."

"Do you think I should get stitches?"

———•◦•———

"One of my fake nails came off and I need a
doctor to get it out of my nose."

———•◦•———

"I accidentally stuck my tongue in an electric outlet
and I got a nasty shock."

———•◦•———

"I feel a cold coming on. I think it should be
here by about twelve."

———•◦•———

"I might have brucellosis. The tests will
be back next week."

"Heatstroke, backstroke . . . something like that."

———•◦•———

"Those cell-phone microwaves must
have cooked my brain."

———•◦•———

"I was impaired by the secondhand smoke
from my grandmother's cigars."

———•◦•———

"A little known fact: men get PMS, too."

———•◦•———

"My boyfriend hit me over the head with a speaker."

———•◦•———

"I couldn't find my dentures."

"I can't make it for the next couple of days.
My leg's in Cambodia."

———•◆•———

"I have hemorrhoids."

———•◆•———

"I was sleepwalking."

———•◆•———

"I blacked out—what happened?"

———•◆•———

"Chemical imbalance."

———•◆•———

"I have chronic fatigue synd—zzzzzzzzzz."

"I think this eye is history."

———•—•———

"I have eye trouble—I just can't see working today."

———•—•———

"There's a boil on my left buttock and it's ready to burst."

———•—•———

"I had a headache the size of Toledo."

———•—•———

"I contracted malaria when I was in Malaysia last year and it's returned for a visit."

———•—•———

"Had to be rushed to hospital for coffee burns on my lap!"

"When I got up this morning, I took two Ex-Lax in addition to my Prozac. I can't get off the toilet, but I feel good about it."

———•◦•———

"I have to deliver a specimen to the doctor's office, but nothing has happened so far."

———•◦•———

"I'm trying to pass a stone."

———•◦•———

"I've had my contact lenses in backward all morning!"

———•◦•———

"I dropped a thirty-pound frozen halibut on my foot."

———•◦•———

"I've got a touch of diarr—oh, call you back."

"I fell asleep in the sun yesterday. The sunburn is so bad, all I can do is walk around naked."

———•◆•———

"I can't work today—I came down with a bad case of something or other."

———•◆•———

"I once worked as a full-time sparring partner."

———•◆•———

"My outpatient surgery went longer than expected."

———•◆•———

"I didn't want to be late for work again, so I'm calling in sick instead."

———•◆•———

"I have worms. Long ones."

"I think I've come down with twenty-four-hour Ebola.
It's going around."

———•◦•———

"Tuna-burrito special is a really bad idea."

———•◦•———

Misery, Yes—But Not Yours

Can't think of an ailment for yourself? Blame your
inefficiencies on someone else's. The less verifiable,
the better.

"Erica has consumption and the doctors want
to observe her."

———•◦•———

"My wife's breasts are sore and I need to stay
home to massage them."

———•◦•———

"I need to help my roommate find his finger."

"Umm, my third cousin's wife has a hangnail.
I'm really worried."

———•◦•———

"My cousin has come to visit on leave from
the leper colony."

———•◦•———

"My wife needs help with her bunions."

———•◦•———

"My husband is still recovering from the vasectomy."

———•◦•———

"The family is taking the cat off life support today."

———•◦•———

"We think Sheila is allergic to your cologne."

"My aunt is flying in from Cleveland. She only has one arm and two pieces of luggage so she really needs me to help her."

———•———

"My sister is trying to dry out and needs a place to get the shakes."

———•———

"I have to stay close to John. With everybody drinking, he might fall off the wagon."

———•———

"My friend was hit by a bus, riding his bike home from the organic food store."

———•———

"We're doing a family intervention today to pry my brother away from a cult."

"My wife said she is going to conceive today, and
I want to be there when it happens."

———

"The old man wears a pacemaker. You've got way
too many microwaves in the house."

———

"My cousin had a terrible tango accident, and
I have to give her a sponge bath."

———

"I can't go anywhere while my sister is in her
sixteen-year-old floozy personality."

———

"My nephew is on the neighbor's roof again."

———

"The Exorcist. Pea soup. Not pretty."

Better Excuses Through Chemicals

> *"I'm on a pharmaceutical cocktail that*
> *would make your liver weep."*

The simple fact is that official-sounding words and terms make it appear that you are telling the truth—unless you're calling in sick to a doctor's office. With an eye toward establishing unquestionable legitimacy, following is a list of medications to work into your excuses. Just mention the names of some of these, and people will be happy not to see you!

Pain Relievers

Over-the-counter
Aspirin: Bufferin, Ascriptin, Ecotrin
Acetaminophen: Anacin-4, Tylenol, Datril
Ibuprofen: Advil, Motrin, Nuprin

Prescription
Codeine, Demerol, Dilaudid, Dolophine, Percodan, Percocet, Numorphan

Antibiotics

Over-the-counter
Neosporin, Polysporin, Neomixin, Lanabiotic, Mycitracin, Bacitracin, Baciguent

Prescription

Achromycin, Amoxicillin, Ampicillin, Aureomycin, Penicillin, Methicillin, Cefazolin, Erythromycin, Enoxacin, Neomycin, Streptomycin, Methacycline, Tetracycline

Antidiarrheals

Over-the-counter

Pepto-Bismol, Kaopectate, Imodium AD

Prescription

Lomotil, Motofen

Antihistamines

Over-the-counter

Allermax, Benadryl, Aller-Chlor, Chlor-Trimeton, Antihist, Tavist 1, Claritin

Prescription

Atrovent, Beconase, Vancenase, Rhinocort, Crolom, Allegra, Clarinex, Zyrtec

Medicine + Obscurity = Excuse

*"I'm sorry about that, but I'm recovering
from that blepharoplasty."*

Let's say you forget to file a really important report that your boss reminded you of five times in the last week. Your job is on the line. "I'm afraid I stored that in the part of the brain they removed in the lobotomy," you say. Baffled and embarrassed, your boss shuffles away to figure out what the hell you just said. He may want to fire you, but he's not sure he can. Such is the impact of using (semi-) obscure medical procedures in an excuse. But use them wisely—if your boss or anyone else knows what rhinoplasty is, they'll notice with a glance that you did not, in fact, recently have surgery on your nose.

Angioplasty: The process of repairing blood vessels, usually used to address clogged arteries.

Appendectomy: The surgical removal of the appendix.

Blepharoplasty: Plastic surgery on the eyelids.

Colposcopy: The use of a special lighted microscope to magnify the cervix during a pelvic examination.

Craniotomy: The surgery performed to open part of the cranium, or skull.

Gastrostomy: The process of inserting a tube into the stomach through the abdomen for feeding or to keep the stomach empty.

Hyperalimentation: Giving nutrients and vitamins to an individual through a vein because they cannot consume the substances themselves.

Mastopexy: The procedure performed to lift the breasts.

Lithotripsy: The procedure used to break up kidney stones into small pieces so that they may be passed from the kidneys.

Lobotomy: A surgical incision in the frontal lobe of the brain to sever nerve fibers; formerly used to treat mental disorders, it is now rarely performed.

Pyloroplasty: A procedure used to widen the opening between the stomach and the small intestine.

Rhinoplasty: Plastic surgery on the nose.

Septoplasty: A plastic surgery procedure used to straighten the nasal septum.

Sigmoidoscopy: The procedure used to examine the lower portions of the large intestine, or colon.

Ventriculoperitoneal Shunt: The insertion of catheters into the ventricles of the brain to drain excess fluid from the brain into the abdomen.

Diseases They'll Have to Look Up

> *"My doctor says it is the worst case of*
> *Minamata disease he's ever seen."*

The more your excuse includes existing medical terminology, the more legitimate it will sound. Particularly effective in instilling fear in coworkers are diseases recently covered in the news. Imagine the fun you'll have and the stories you can tell after your boss says, in his best "I'm concerned" voice, "Well, I hope you get over your Werner syndrome soon."

African Trypanosomiasis: Also known as African sleeping sickness, this hard-to-pronounce illness is transmitted by tsetse flies and is identified by pain, headaches, and fever, followed later by confusion, poor coordination, and interruption of the sleep cycle (hence the name).

Beriberi: The primary cause of this particular illness is vitamin deficiency, primarily of thiamine, in the body. But the most common reason for this thiamine shortfall is excessive alcohol consumption.

Bovine Spongiform Encephalopathy (BSE): As a human, you cannot get this affliction, better known as mad cow disease. However, eating meat from cattle infected with BSE could result in variant Creutzfeldt-Jakob Disease.

Creutzfeldt-Jakob Disease (CJD): This is a rare illness that usually manifests later in life and gradually deteriorates the brain, causing dementia and loss of coordination and memory. This disease is one in a family of diseases called transmissible spongiform encephalopathies (TSEs).

Dengue Fever: A disease of the tropics carried by mosquitoes, dengue can appear as a nonspecific viral infection or a very serious hemorrhagic (profuse bleeding) disease.

Ebola Virus: Once much more prominent in the popular consciousness, Ebola has faded from the news over recent years, primarily because it did not wipe out the human species as feared. Even though initial concerns may have been overblown, Ebola is a nasty little disease that claims most of those afflicted and is characterized by flulike symptoms, followed by internal and external bleeding.

Leishmaniasis: This particular tropical affliction comes in two forms: cutaneous and visceral. The disease is spread by the bites of infected sand flies and is characterized either by volcano-like open sores (cutaneous), or by fever, weight loss, and an enlarged spleen and liver (visceral).

Marburg Virus: Similar in symptoms to the Ebola virus, Marburg is most often transmitted to humans through contact with infected monkeys (as is Ebola), even though monkeys are not the disease's natural host. From human to human, both Marburg and Ebola are transmitted through contact with infected blood.

Minamata Disease: This strange illness emerged in Japan in the 1950s. It stems from mercury poisoning as a result of environmental pollution. The offending corporation that introduced the disease and the Japanese government were held liable in a legal case.

Monkey Pox: Similar to smallpox and (unsurprisingly) originating in Africa, monkey pox manifests in headache, backache, fever, and swollen lymph nodes. Though very rare, this particular virus has made an appearance in the U.S.

Mycosis Fungoides: This is the most common of a group of rare skin cancers.

River Blindness: This is caused by parasites invading the body and is characterized by itching, lesions, and, quite frequently, blindness.

Severe Acute Respiratory Syndrome (SARS): Well known by now, thanks to recent scares, SARS looks initially like a common viral infection and often develops into pneumonia.

Tolosa-Hunt Syndrome: Characterized by extreme pain around or behind one eye, followed by double vision and numbness of the forehead, Tolosa-Hunt can be alleviated using steroids, but the changes to vision may persist.

Werner Syndrome: The most common of the "early aging" disorders, sufferers of Werner syndrome develop in their thirties the gray air, wrinkled face, cataracts, and osteoporosis common to much older individuals.

West Nile Virus: This is another mosquito-borne disease. The overwhelming majority of people infected with West Nile will show no symptoms whatsoever. Some, however, will suffer muscle fatigue, headache, stiffness, disorientation, convulsions, coma, paralysis, and loss of vision.

Nonsensical Syndromes

Obscure and exotic diseases aren't the only material you can use in creative excuse making. You can also use ridiculous and outlandish syndromes—other people have. Purportedly, each of the excuses that follow were first identified by a reputable medical journal or mentioned in a newspaper, but one can never be sure.

Air-traffic Controller's Syndrome: Peptic ulcers occurring among air-traffic controllers as a result of job stress. [*Illinois Medical Journal,* 1972]

Alopecia Walkmania: Loss of hair from prolonged use of personal stereo headphones. [*Journal of the American Medical Association (JAMA),* 1984]

Anchorman Glaze: Glazed-eye look of TV anchormen caused by looking at the TelePromptR through glaring camera lights. [Syracuse, New York, TV station, 1960]

Arctic Temper: Extreme irritability developing among arctic explorers exposed to darkness, monotony, isolation, and sensory deprivation. [*The Lancet,* 1910]

Beer Drinker's Finger: Swelling, bluish discoloration, and wasting of finger caused by placing pop-top beer-can rings on finger. [*JAMA,* 1968]

Bingo Brain: The headache associated with carbon-monoxide intoxication that occurs after spending long hours in smoke-filled bingo halls. [Canadian Medical Conference, 1982]

Birdwatcher's Twitch: The nervous and prolonged excitement of spotting a species for the first time. [*New Scientist*, 1982]

Bodybuilder's Psychosis: Psychotic episodes associated with the use of anabolic steroids, causing hallucinations, paranoid delusions, grandiose beliefs, and manic-depressive symptoms. [*The Lancet*, 1987]

Bookseller's Bends: Sickness caused by changes in atmospheric pressure because the book the customer wants is always on the top shelf. [*New England Medical Monthly*, 1974]

Casino Feet: Soreness of the feet caused by standing in front of slot machines for long periods of time. [Wilmington *Morning Star*, 1981]

Chicken Neck Wringer's Finger: Partial dislocation and arthritis of middle finger joint from continued use of this finger to dislocate chicken necks for slaughtering. [*British Medical Cooperative Journal*, 1955]

Christmas Depression: Psychological stress during the holidays, related to the use of alcohol and to social pressures. [*JAMA*, 1982]

Credit Card-itis: Pain over the rear and down the thigh due to pressure on the nerve from a wallet stuffed with credit cards. [*New England Medical Monthly*, 1966]

Disco Digit: A sore finger from snapping fingers while dancing. [*New England Medical Monthly*, 1976]

Dog Walker's Elbow: Pain caused by constant tension and tugs from a dog leash. [*New England Medical Monthly*, 1979]

Electronic Space-War Video-Game Epilepsy: Epilepsy caused by the flashing lights of electronic video games. [*British Medical Cooperative Journal*, 1982]

Espresso Wrist: Pain from strong wrist motions made by espresso-machine operators required to make the coffee. [*JAMA*, 1956]

Flip-flop Dermatitis: Skin disease of the feet from wearing rubber flip-flops. [*British Medical Cooperative Journal*, 1965]

Frisbee Finger: Cutting of finger from strenuous throwing of a Frisbee. [*New England Medical Monthly*, 1975]

Golf Arm: Shoulder and elbow pain from too many rounds of golf. [*British Medical Cooperative Journal*, 1896]

Hooker's Elbow: Painful shoulder and upper-arm swelling suffered by fishermen from repeatedly jerking upward on fishing line. [*New England Medical Monthly*, 1981]

Housewife-itis: Nervous symptoms related to spending too much time managing a busy household. [*Centreview*, 1976]

Humper's Lump: Swelling suffered by hotel porters from lugging heavy bags. [*Diseases of Occupations*, 1975]

Ice-cream Frostbite: Frostbite and blackening of the lips from prolonged contact with ice cream. [*New England Medical Monthly*, 1982]

Jazz Ballet Bottom: Painful abscesses suffered by dancers who frequently spin on their bottoms. [*British Medical Cooperative Journal*, 1987]

Jeans Folliculitis: Irritation of the hair follicles from the waist to the knees caused by ultratight jeans. [*New England Medical Monthly*, 1981]

Joystick Digit: Trigger-finger pain following prolonged use of video-game joysticks. [*JAMA*, 1987]

Knife-Sharpener's Cramp: Painful hand swelling from sharpening too many knives. [Diseases of Occupations, 1975]

Label Licker's Tongue: Ulcers in mouth from sensitivity to sticky labels. [*Dangerous Trades*, 1902]

Money Counter's Cramp: Painful seizure of muscles from counting too much cash. [*English Press*, 1975]

Motorway Blues: The sort of headaches noted by drivers on congested motorways. [*British Medical Cooperative Journal*, 1963]

Nun's Knee: Swelling of kneecap from repeated kneeling in prayer. [Diseases of Occupations, 1975]

Oyster Shucker's Keratitis: Eye irritation from contact with fragments of oyster shells. [*British Medical Cooperative Journal*, 1896]

Panty Girdle Syndrome: Tingling or swelling of feet from wearing a too-tight panty girdle. [*British Medical Cooperative Journal*, 1972]

Player's Liver: The hazard of spending too much time in the bar instead of playing the game. [*Encyclopedia of Sports*, 1971]

Quick-Draw Leg: Bullet wound in the leg from practicing the quick draw of a gun from a belt holster. [*JAMA*, 1966]

Reflex Horn Syndrome: Tendency of drivers waiting in traffic jams to toot horns. [*New England Medical Monthly*, 1976]

Retired Husband Syndrome: Tension, headaches, depression, and anxiety felt by women whose husbands have just retired. [*Western Health Journal*, 1984]

Seamstress's Bottom: Hardening of skin following long-term trauma from rocking on the hips while operating a sewing machine. [*American Family Physician*, 1979]

Sick Santa Syndrome: Lower back pain from lifting heavy children and parcels; acquired illnesses from multiple contacts with kids. [*JAMA*, 1986]

Television Legs: Loss of normal flexibility of the legs from being slumped in a chair in front of the idiot box for too long. [*JAMA*, 1958]

Toilet Seat Dermatitis: Skin irritation on rear from spending too much time on the toilet. [*Ugeskr Laeger*, 1980]

Uniform Rash: Skin irritation of the neck, chest, and arms from wearing new uniforms. [*British Medical Cooperative Journal*, 1973]

Volkswagen Dermatitis: Allergic skin reaction caused by rubber bumper guards. [*Dermatological Archive*, 1971]

Working Wife Syndrome: Fatigue, irritability, headaches, and diminished sex drive from the strain of doing two jobs. [*Lancet*, 1966]

Yoga Foot Drop: Paralysis of foot due to compounded pressure from practicing yoga positions. [*JAMA*, 1971]

The Meteorological Excuse

"Can you believe this weather we're having?"

The meteorological excuse—that's fancy for blaming it on the weather. There are those among you—and you know exactly who you are—who long for a cloudy, rainy, or snowy day because of the opportunities to excuse yourself it will afford you. While less effective than the medical excuse, this option is a little easier to pull off.

> "My car hydroplaned into a McDonald's—I'm waiting for a tow truck and some fries."

> "The storm blew a mailbox and two Mormon missionaries through our front window."

> "A meteorite the size of a grapefruit ripped through our roof, tore through the bed between the two of us, and continued through the floor into the basement. We're a little shell-shocked today."

"I have rainaphobia really bad. I can't leave until it stops."

———•·•———

"The freezing rain glued my car to the road."

———•·•———

"I licked a snowflake off my hand and my tongue stuck to my finger."

———•·•———

"I was groping around for candles and knocked a bottle of wine off the shelf. My wife found me when the power came back on."

———•·•———

"With all this humidity, the front door was swollen shut."

———•·•———

"My barometric pressure has been dropping all week."

"I got caught in the jet stream."

———•◆•———

"It's so foggy in here I couldn't see the phone."

———•◆•———

"My tongue was stuck to the neighbor's metal fence."

———•◆•———

"I dropped my keys in the snow and I'm waiting
for it to warm up so I can find them."

———•◆•———

"The TV weatherman advised me to stay indoors."

———•◆•———

"It's so hot my denture glue keeps melting!"

"I'm afraid to leave the house when it's foggy."

———•·•———

"A hurricane formed in my kid's wading pool."

———•·•———

"I've been depressed over global warming."

———•·•———

"I need to put an aftermarket periscope on my car."

———•·•———

"I'm taking the temperature inversion very personally."

———•·•———

"I was struck by lightning—I can power
the city all by myself."

"A five-pound icicle fell off the roof and
pinned me to the dog."

———•·•———

"There was a leak in the mailbox and
all our bills floated away."

———•·•———

"I took that wind-chill advisory very seriously!"

———•·•———

"It was foggy and I missed the building."

———•·•———

"There are snow flurries inside my cranium."

———•·•———

"I went to leave and a tornado had moved my car."

"It was so cloudy in my house, I couldn't
find the way out."

———•◦•———

"There was a flash flood in my bathroom."

———•◦•———

"There's six feet of snow and I'm digging
out the car with a spatula."

———•◦•———

"I need to help lift a house off this old
witch who lives down the street."

———•◦•———

"There was a red sky this morning, and I'm
sort of a sailor at heart."

The Proverbial Excuse

"Helping hands are best kept in pockets."

The thing about proverbs, maxims, and axioms is that they sound wise. Using them as excuses will make some feel like you've thought long and hard about what you're saying, while others will wonder if they've missed something. Use this to your advantage.

"Convictions are more dangerous enemies
of truth than lies."

———•◦•———

"They also serve who stand and wait."

———•◦•———

"Always trust, but also remember to
tie your camel to the post."

———•◦•———

"Fame is a powerful aphrodisiac."

"Sweets grown common
lose their dear delight."

"Fashions are but induced epidemics."

"A bad beginning makes a bad ending."

"The devil finds work for idle hands."

"By working faithfully eight hours a day, you
may get to be a boss and work twelve."

"Harmony seldom makes a headline."

"A fool and his money are soon parted."

———•◦•———

"I have nothing to declare but my genius."

———•◦•———

"Fools rush in where angels fear to tread."

———•◦•———

"Praise the sea, but stay on the land."

———•◦•———

"Have no friends not equal to thyself."

———•◦•———

"There is nothing in this world constant
but inconstancy."

"Honor wears different coats to different eyes."

———•—•———

"Anything will fit a naked man."

———•—•———

"There is pain in prohibition."

———•—•———

"What you don't know can't hurt you."

———•—•———

"Nothing is inevitable until it happens."

———•—•———

"The art of living is more like
wrestling than dancing."

"There is more to life than increasing its speeed."

———•·•———

"Life is ours to be spent, not saved."

———•·•———

"Money lent is an enemy made."

———•·•———

"Revenge is profitable; gratitude is expensive."

———•·•———

"When manna falls from heaven, take a bite."

———•·•———

"Only dull people are brilliant at breakfast."

———•·•———

"Fame is proof that people are gullible."

"Competitions are for horses, not artists."

———•—•—

"Punctuality is the virtue of the bored."

———•—•—

"Everyone must row with the oars he has."

———•—•—

"Modest dogs miss much meat."

———•—•—

"He who climbs not high will fall not far."

———•—•—

"In wine there is truth."

———•—•—

"A tree falls the way it leans."

"Lend your money and
lose your friend."

"A rose too often smelled loses
its fragrance."

"There's none so blind as they
that don't see."

"Effective action is always unjust."

"When angry count four.
When very angry, swear."

"Heaven for climate. Hell for society."

"What costs little is worth little."

———•◦•———

"What use is coffee without donuts?"

———•◦•———

"Vulgarity is the garlic
in the salad of taste."

———•◦•———

"Past hope, past cure, past help."

———•◦•———

"Failure is the opportunity
to begin again."

———•◦•———

"Running away is not cowardice,
but wisdom."

The Nonsensical Excuse

"I'd love to, but . . ."

Do you care whether friends, family, and colleagues see you as lucid and responsible? If not, you can avoid certain obligations and situations by using one of the following excuses. Each absurd statement can leave that special someone happy you declined their invitation.

"I have to floss my cat."

———•◆•———

"The man on television told me to say tuned."

———•◆•———

"I want to spend more time with my blender."

———•◆•———

"The president said he might drop in."

"I've been scheduled for a karma transplant."

———•◆•———

"I'm staying home to work on my
cottage-cheese sculpture."

———•◆•———

"It's my parakeet's bowling night."

———•◆•———

"I've dedicated my life to linguini."

———•◆•———

"It wouldn't be fair to the
other Beautiful People."

"The march to war hurt the economy. Laura
reminded me a while ago that remember
what was on the TV screens—she calls
me, 'George W.'—'George W.' I call her,
'First Lady.' No, anyway—she said, we said,
march to war on our TV screen."

—*President George W. Bush*

"I'm building a pig from a kit."

"I'm enrolled in aerobic scream therapy."

"I have to check the freshness dates on my dairy products."

"I'm going through cherry-cheesecake withdrawal."

"I did my own thing and
now I've got to undo it."

———•◦•———

"I'm planning to go downtown
to try on gloves."

———•◦•———

"My crayons all melted together."

———•◦•———

"I'm trying to see how long I can go
without saying yes."

———•◦•———

"I'm in training to be a household pest."

———•◦•———

"I'm getting my overalls overhauled."

"I had to give my plasma TV an infusion."

"My patent is pending."

"I'm only human. Well, actually,
I'm half three-toed tree sloth."

"You have tiny hands and tiny feet."

"I'm attending the opening of my
garage door."

"I'm sandblasting my oven."

"I'm worried about my vertical hold."

—•—

"I'm going down to the bakery to
watch the buns rise."

—•—

"I'm being deported."

—•—

"I'm going door-to-door, collecting
for static cling."

—•—

"I have to go to the post office to see
if I'm still wanted."

—•—

"The grunion are running."

"I'll be looking for a parking space."

———•◦•———

"My Millard Filmore Fan Club meets then."

———•◦•———

"The monsters haven't turned blue yet, and I
have to eat more dots."

———•◦•———

"I made an appointment with a cuticle specialist."

———•◦•———

"My plot to take over the world is thickening."

———•◦•———

"I have to fulfill my potential."

"I don't want to leave my comfort zone."

"It's too close to the turn of the century."

"I have some real hard words to
look up in the dictionary."

"My subconscious says no."

"I'm attending a perfume convention
as guest sniffer."

"My yucca plant is feeling yucky."

"I'm touring China with a wok band."

———•◦•———

"My chocolate-appreciation class meets that night."

———•◦•———

"I never go out on days that end in Y."

———•◦•———

"I'm giving nuisance lessons at a convenience store."

———•◦•———

"I left my body in my other clothes."

———•◦•———

"The last time I went,
I never came back."

"I've got a Friends of Rutabaga meeting."

"I'm taking punk totem-pole carving."

"I have to fluff my shower cap."

"I'm converting my calendar watch from Julian to Gregorian."

"I have to answer all of my 'occupant' letters."

"None of my socks match."

"I'm making a home movie called
The Thing That Grew in My Refrigerator."

———•◦•———

"My mother would never let me hear the end of it."

———•◦•———

"I'm running off to Yugoslavia with a foreign-exchange
student named Basil Metabolism."

———•◦•———

"I just picked up a book called *Glue in Many Lands* and I
can't put it down."

———•◦•———

"I'm uncomfortable when I'm alone or with others."

———•◦•———

"I promised to help a friend fold road maps."

"I feel a song coming on."

———•◆•———

"I have to be on the next
train to Bermuda."

———•◆•———

"I'm having all my plants neutered."

———•◆•———

"People are blaming me for the
Spanish-American War."

———•◆•———

"I changed the lock on my door and
now I can't get out."

———•◆•———

"I'm trying to be less popular."

"My bathroom tiles need grouting."

———•◦•———

"I have too much guilt."

———•◦•———

"There are important world issues
that need worrying about."

———•◦•———

"I have to draw Cubby for an art scholarship."

———•◦•———

"I have to bleach my hare."

———•◦•———

"I'm waiting to see if I'm already a winner."

"I'm writing a love letter to
Richard Simmons."

———•◦•———

"I'm observing National Apathy Week."

———•◦•———

"I have to rotate my crops."

———•◦•———

"My uncle escaped again."

———•◦•———

"I'm up to my elbows in waxy buildup."

———•◦•———

"I have to knit some dust bunnies
for a charity bazaar."

"I have to stay home and see if I snore."

———•◦•———

"You know how we psychos are."

———•◦•———

"My favorite commercial
is on TV."

———•◦•———

"I have to study for a blood test."

———•◦•———

"I'm going to be old someday."

———•◦•———

"I've been traded to Cincinnati."

"I prefer to remain an enigma."

———•◆•———

"I have to sit up with a sick ant."

———•◆•———

"I'm having my baby shoes bronzed."

———•◆•———

"I have to go to court for kitty littering."

———•◆•———

"I'm going to count the bristles
in my toothbrush."

———•◆•———

"I have to thaw some karate chops for dinner."

"Having fun gives me prickly heat."

———•———

"I'm going to the Missing Persons Bureau to see if anyone is looking for me."

———•———

"I have to jog my memory."

———•———

"My palm reader advised against it."

———•———

"My Dress for Obscurity class meets then."

———•———

"I'm drunk on Jesus and I don't care who knows!"

For Wage Slaves

*"I don't know what's wrong.
But I know it's not my fault!"*

Whatever happens at work—whether you've failed to accomplish anything, show up, stay awake at your desk, or stay off the Internet—you can always find someone or something to blame it on.

Lateness and Absenteeism Are Grounds for Dismissal

"I ate a huge plate of rancid kimchee and can't leave the bathroom."

———•◦•———

"My doctor insisted I slow down."

———•◦•———

"This constipation has made me a walking time bomb."

"I have a chance of filling in
for someone on jury duty."

———•———

"My mother is one of the undead.
We need to find her and drive a stake
through her heart."

———•———

"My head was lodged in the microwave again."

———•———

"I just found out I was switched at birth,
so all my records contain false information."

———•———

"The voices told me to stay home and
clean the guns today."

"I'm stuck in the blood-pressure machine
down at the Safeway."

———•◆•———

"I'm stalking my previous boss, who fired
me for not showing up for work."

———•◆•———

"The dog ate my car keys. We're going to
hitchhike to the vet's office."

———•◆•———

"I fell on the soap in the shower and
I need to have it dislodged."

———•◆•———

"It's a Jewish holiday today—we remember the life of
David ben Goldbricker."

"I have an interview for a job I really want
and cannot be bothered to lie."

———•◆•———

"My darling donkey, Muriel, finally
lost her battle with emphysema."

———•◆•———

"I thought today was Thanksgiving."

———•◆•———

"I was lost in the Bermuda Triangle!"

———•◆•———

"I was there.
Where the hell were you?"

———•◆•———

"I'm using the Julian calendar."

"Haste makes waste."

———•◦•———

"I just realized this morning I'm still using
last year's calendar."

———•◦•———

"Someone left a baby in a basket on our doorstep.
I've been at the police station."

———•◦•———

"Gypsies stole my pants!"

———•◦•———

"I'm on Hawaii time during the morning.
In the afternoon I'll revert back to local time."

———•◦•———

"I wanted to avoid looking eager."

"My neighbor's house is blocking my driveway."

⎯⎯•◦•⎯⎯

"I fell down a manhole, and the water
swept me along for two blocks before
I could grab a ladder. When I climbed out
I smelled so foul I had to go right
back home and take a bath."

⎯⎯•◦•⎯⎯

"The lights were against me."

⎯⎯•◦•⎯⎯

"But I've never been late this early before!"

⎯⎯•◦•⎯⎯

"I was delayed at a yak crossing."

"I went to a concert last night.
This morning I couldn't even hear the alarm."

———•••———

"I didn't think that time was literal."

———•••———

"It took longer than I expected to trim my nose hair."

———•••———

"I forgot we went off daylight saving time."

———•••———

"My alarm is participating in an industry-wide strike."

———•••———

"Mick told me time was on my side."

"I thought it was spring forward and fall back."

———•◦•———

"I stopped to help an eighty-year-old woman load a refrigerator onto a truck."

———•◦•———

"My mom overslept this morning."

———•◦•———

"I like to make a grand entrance."

———•◦•———

"Someone moved my apartment building while I was sleeping."

———•◦•———

"My watch is narcoleptic."

"I was halfway here when the fly on my pants
just busted open."

———•◆•———

"I came down with jet lag this morning."

———•◆•———

"A column of leafcutter ants was crossing the road."

———•◆•———

"There was a *Mr. Belvedere* marathon on TV."

———•◆•———

"I got pulled over for driving with expired milk."

———•◆•———

"I was listening to someone tell me
wonderful things about you."

"I'm still drunk from last night."

—•—

"My left-turn blinker is broken—I had to
make right turns all the way here."

—•—

"The squirrels are too tired to start the car."

—•—

"The printer just committed a felony."

—•—

"My cell phone destroyed too many brain cells."

—•—

"We got the I Love You virus,
but it isn't very romantic."

"Microsoft help desk. For three hours.
I don't feel helped."

———•◦•———

"My PDA went AWOL."

———•◦•———

"Either my watch stopped or the earth
started rotating the other way."

———•◦•———

"I've decided to become a Luddite."

———•◦•———

"I just can't seem to navigate shoelaces."

———•◦•———

"It took me thirty minutes to get the
top off the orange juice."

"My grinder broke and I had to crush
coffee beans by hand."

———•◦•———

"The elevator held me hostage and demanded a ransom."

———•◦•———

"I was surrounded by my sound system."

———•◦•———

"My GPS has a sense of humor."

———•◦•———

"Somebody activated the ballistic missile
silo under my house."

———•◦•———

"The shower broke—I had to figure out
how to take a bath."

"I got my tongue caught in the coffee vending machine."

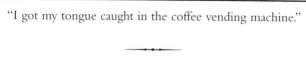

"I got into a heated argument with the ATM."

"I overcharged my cell phone and it electrocuted me."

The Only Good Replacement for Competence

"The low morale got to me."

"This is part of my grand plan."

"I accidentally wore my iPod into the shower."

"I didn't want to make everyone else
look so incompetent!"

———•◦•———

"Didn't you get the memo?"

———•◦•———

"That is really contrary to the mission statement."

———•◦•———

"Just making sure you're paying attention."

———•◦•———

"I was testing your ability to not be a dickhead."

———•◦•———

"I never got the memo."

"Asking me to do this really displays a lack of wisdom on your part."

———•———

"Someone else was using the pencil."

—*Dorothy Parker, explaining to her* New Yorker *editor why she had spent the afternoon in a bar instead of her office*

———•———

"My wastebasket caught fire."

———•———

"I'm very, very sensitive to rising interest rates."

———•———

"This cubicle really stifles my creativity."

———•———

"I haven't been eating enough possum lately."

"I would like to remain an enigma."

———•••———

"I wanted to avoid looking like a brown-noser."

———•••———

"My laptop swore at me. I think our
relationship is troubled."

———•••———

"I can't read my own writing."

———•••———

"I'm not much of a follower."

———•••———

"I'm not a very good leader."

"Well, Jim, *The Sound of Music* was on last night."

—*President Ronald Reagan, explaining to Chief of Staff Jim Baker why he hadn't had time to prepare for an economic summit*

"The incompetence gene is recessive in my family, but I got it."

"I was role-playing an idiotic failure."

"I'm too old for this."

"I'm too young for this."

"It was the caffeine talking."

———•◦•———

"This new underwear is cutting off my circulation."

———•◦•———

"The buck stops on her desk—yeah,
over by the wall."

———•◦•———

"We drew straws—I got to screw up this time."

———•◦•———

"*Siesta*" is Spanish for *seminar*.

———•◦•———

"I decided to work smarter, not harder."

"These office colors are depressing my consciousness."

———•◆•———

"Actually, I was testing the keyboard for drool resistance."

———•◆•———

"They told me at the blood bank this might happen."

———•◆•———

"It depends on your definition of asleep.
They weren't stretched out.
They had their eyes closed.
They were seated at their desks
with their heads in a nodding position."

—*John Hogan, Commonwealth Edison spokesperson,*
on an allegation that Dresden Nuclear Power
Plant workers were sleeping on the job

———•◆•———

"You can't just come into my milieu like that."

"This is one of the seven habits of
highly effective people."

———•◦•———

"Damn it, why did you interrupt me?
I'd almost solved our most difficult problem!"

———•◦•———

"Actually, this was just one of those
fifteen-minute power naps they raved about
in that last time-management course you sent me to."

———•◦•———

"My laptop refuses to start up unless
I reinstall Tomb Raider."

———•◦•———

"I have a really slow metabolism."

"This is a highly specific yoga exercise designed to
relieve work-related stress."

———•◦•———

"Whew, I must have left the top off the Liquid Paper."

———•◦•———

"Boy, that cold medicine I took last night
just won't wear off."

———•◦•———

"I have the words already. What I'm seeking is
the perfect order of words in the sentence."

—*James Joyce, on why it was taking him
so long to finish* Ulysses

———•◦•———

"In Jesus' name, amen."

"The coffee machine is busted."

———•◦•———

"Someone made decaf in the wrong pot."

———•◦•———

"Ah, the unique and unpredictable circadian rhythms of the workaholic."

———•◦•———

"I wasn't sleeping. I was trying to pick up a contact lens without using my hands."

———•◦•———

"I was researching the competition."

Been Caught Surfing

The Internet is either the greatest technological advancement in recent memory or the most debilitating temptation ever faced by the average employee. Could it be both? So, if the World Wide Wormhole pulls you in, be prepared when your manager happens to wander by.

"I was trying to establish a link with reality."

———•◦•———

"It's a virus."

———•◦•———

"I think Microsoft programmed it to do this."

———•◦•———

"Overwhelming sunspot activity."

———•◦•———

"Somebody tied a knot in my Ethernet cable."

"There's a compatibility problem between
the mouse and my hand."

———•◦•———

"These fluorescent lights must be
creating negative ions."

———•◦•———

"I think the server needs more Prozac."

———•◦•———

"I think my computer may have had unsafe sex."

———•◦•———

"I tried to shift paradigms without using the clutch."

———•◦•———

"The server has a nasty addiction."

"I think the Borg have assimilated the system."

"Communists took over the server and
are threatening to shoot the administrators."

"I'm using these sites to do that anatomy
research you asked for."

"We've got dyslexics typing the host files into the server."

"French above-ground nuclear testing."

"That firewall has really gotten toasty!"

"I had to use a hammer earlier on the disk drive."

———•—•———

"The help desk changed my default home page to Playboy.com."

———•—•———

"My Java is really cold."

———•—•———

"I'm testing my monitor to make sure it gets all four million colors."

———•—•———

"Yes, I'm playing a game. We're a gaming company!"

———•—•———

"I don't think my browser understands English."

For Desk-Bound Youth

"I was staging a sit-in demanding better teachers' salaries."

You've got your work cut out for you here—teachers have heard them all. But scientific studies by those researchers in white lab coats have proven that the more creative and amusing the excuse given a teacher, the better the chance the excuse-maker will get off.

The Bell Tolls for Thee

"I have a note from my mother. I have a note from my doctor. I have a note from my mother's doctor."

———

"The president asks that you excuse me for the time he required my help."

———

"I lost my eraser. I had to stay home to find it."

———

"I wanted to see if the class could go on without me."

"I didn't want the classroom to be so crowded."

———•◦•———

"I was visiting relatives from the homeland."

———•◦•———

"I thought Groundhog Day
was a national holiday."

———•◦•———

"My pantyhose blew a gasket."

———•◦•———

"I'm addicted to Pong."

———•◦•———

"The alarm clock is tired of trying."

"I squeezed too much toothpaste out of the tube
and it took me a while to get it back in."

———•◦•———

"You know what they say . . .
absence makes the heart grow fonder!"

———•◦•———

"I was afraid I would forget everything
I learned at home."

———•◦•———

"Wasn't there a teacher's strike yesterday?"

———•◦•———

"It must be all the drugs."

———•◦•———

"I couldn't find any matching socks."

"I woke up with an earlobe infection."

———•—•———

"I was walking under a tree and
a walnut knocked me cold."

———•—•———

"I had an accordion lesson."

———•—•———

"I was playing hide-and-seek alone.
I never found myself."

———•—•———

"I had to walk my Chia Pet."

———•—•———

"But I don't feel tardy!"

"I'm punctuality challenged."

"My alarm clock stopped working
when I beat it with a hammer."

"Johnny was late today
because of a shallow gene pool."

"But I'm here early for
tomorrow's class."

"My nose was running.
I had to catch it."

"I recently converted to Hinduism
and there was a cow in the road."

———•◦•———

"Static cling had me stuck to the bed for hours."

———•◦•———

"I was accosted by heavily armed dwarves
who felt vengeful about their lack of stature."

———•◦•———

"I've been freebasing coffee
grounds all morning."

———•◦•———

"My mom makes me milk the
cow every morning."

"I'm late because the bell rang
before I got here!"

———•◆•———

"Didn't you feel the earthquake?"

———•◆•———

"When I got up this morning, my medulla
oblongata just felt really funny."

———•◆•———

"Lateness is in my genes."

———•◆•———

"Don't you think this should be considered
cruel and unusual punishment?"

Delinquent Bibliophiles

You know that kindly middle-aged woman at the library, the one who always smiles and says hello as you enter? It's a ruse. Just lose one of her books and watch Mother Teresa turn into Mother Superior. But you gotta sympathize—just look at the ridiculous excuses she has to endure.

"What book?"

"I'll bring it back as soon as the glue dries."

"I'm not returning that piece of trash to my public library!"

"I went to a book burning last week and it was perfect for the event."

"I took it fishing and it fell overboard."

———•◦•———

"Somebody threw it in the boys' room toilet."

———•◦•———

"My baby brother barfed on it."

———•◦•———

"That cold spell last week caught me
without any firewood."

———•◦•———

"I'm still reading it to elderly shut-ins at the senior center."

———•◦•———

"The FBI is still keeping it as evidence."

"Somebody stole it from my locker."

———•———

"It offended me, so I challenged it to a duel. I won."

———•———

"I haven't finished translating it into Klingon yet."

———•———

"Ray Bradbury was right on with that
whole *Fahrenheit 451* thing."

———•———

"It's a real downer."

—*Members of the Alabama State
Textbook Committee, in a 1983 effort
to explain why* Anne Frank: The Diary
of a Young Girl *should be banned
from public school libraries*

118

"I'm using it to press flowers from the gerbil's funeral."

———•◆•———

"It was stolen by a vicious gang of
black-market book dealers."

———•◆•———

"It went to the same place socks in the dryer go."

———•◆•———

"My mom said I couldn't read it
and threw it away."

———•◆•———

"It's holding up a table in the cellar."

———•◆•———

"It's in Myrtle Beach."

"It's on the bus. I think."

———•◆•———

"You have me confused
with someone literate."

———•◆•———

"I'm not finished blacking out
all the bad words."

———•◆•———

"I used it for origami practice."

———•◆•———

"Spontaneous combustion."

———•◆•———

"The puppy needed something to pee on."

"*The New York Times* called and asked
to borrow it for a review."

———•◦•———

"It was so bad I decided to do the only
responsible thing—recycle it."

———•◦•———

"I'm still memorizing it."

———•◦•———

"God called it home to the great library in the sky."

———•◦•———

"I was out of cigarette paper."

———•◦•———

"It worked well as an emergency umbrella."

"The author took it to make revisions."

———•◦•———

"I'm making photocopies to
resell as my own work."

———•◦•———

When You Don't Have a Dog . . .

"Homework? What homework?"

———•◦•———

"I'm allergic to pencil lead."

———•◦•———

"The English tutor is sick today."

———•◦•———

"I think it was the wedgie."

"Ken Starr confiscated my paper,
'Secret Sex in the White House.'"

———•◦•———

"I had an origami fit—my homework is
now a beautiful swan."

———•◦•———

"Aren't slackers still fashionable?"

———•◦•———

"I have a medical excuse:
homework makes me sick."

———•◦•———

"I was using 'you the shit'
in the hip-hop sense."

———•◦•———

"Brain fart."

"The university empties the recycling
bins at seven A.M."

———◆———

"Homework bandits robbed
me on my way to school."

———◆———

"The finance company was coming to
repossess my parents' television, and
I needed to get in one last night
of watching TV."

———◆———

"My waterbed made me seasick."

———◆———

"I'm just too stupid for this."

"I'm way too smart for this."

———◆◆◆———

"I got caught in a blizzard and had to burn
my homework to stay warm."

———◆◆◆———

"I couldn't do my homework because
it got dark outside."

———◆◆◆———

"I accidentally divided by zero, and my paper
burst into flames."

———◆◆◆———

"That man over there said it was okay.
Well, he was there just a minute ago."

"My science project ate it."

———•◦•———

"My roommate hasn't finished writing it yet."

———•◦•———

"My brother spilled invisible ink all over it."

———•◦•———

"The atomic structure of my essay became unstable,
so it disintegrated."

———•◦•———

"George W. Bush was a lousy student,
and look where it got him!"

———•◦•———

"I'm going to turn it in as soon as my friend
gets it back from his instructor."

"I got cold on the way to school,
so I used it to build a fire."

———•◦•———

"When I tried to run back in to save my homework,
the fireman stopped me."

———•◦•———

"I have a solar-powered calculator and it was cloudy."

———•◦•———

"I sent my only copy to *The New Yorker* for publication."

———•◦•———

"I was supposed to bring it back to school?"

———•◦•———

"My mom spilled her coffee on it,
so I threw it away."

"My mom got caught up in a grease fire,
and I had to smother her with my homework
so that she wouldn't die."

———•·•———

"My little brother drew dirty pictures all over it."

———•·•———

"I did it in my head. Ask me a question."

———•·•———

"The housekeeper must've thrown it out."

———•·•———

"According to feng shui, my homework was
creating a negative energy space on my desk."

———•·•———

"I couldn't find any pencils to write with."

"My lawyer is advising me to respond
'no comment' regarding the whereabouts of my
alleged homework at this time."

———•◦•———

"When you told us how important recycling is,
I took all my books and papers to the
recycling bin right away."

———•◦•———

"When you said multiple-choice exam,
I thought that meant we could choose not to take it."

———•◦•———

"There's an ethnic bias in this test."

———•◦•———

"This isn't a remedial class?
I think we've been going too fast."

"I thought this was going to be an advanced class.
I don't want to go back and study fundamentals again."

———•◦•———

"I'll never use any of this information in a real job."

———•◦•———

"I left my cheat sheet in my locker."

———•◦•———

"I still have memory lapses,
but the school psychologist has really
helped me make progress."

———•◦•———

"I just found out I'm dyslexic.
I'm taking classes in spelling and reading fundamentals."

———•◦•———

"My hormones are running amuck."

"I'm really a visually oriented person,
and you haven't shown enough movies in class."

———•———

"You haven't really motivated me."

———•———

"You know, your approach doesn't really
capture what's happening in the world today."

———•———

"If I'd studied harder, my answers would have
been less spontaneous."

———•———

"I have two mommies."

———•———

"I want to be the child that gets left behind."

"I'm a latchkey kid."

———•◦•———

"I'm a part of Generation X."

———•◦•———

"I blame it on Kurt Cobain."

———•◦•———

"In this economy? What does it matter?"

———•◦•———

"I need God's help to pass,
but you won't let me pray."

———•◦•———

"The cafeteria food is making me ill."

"I ate ice cream so fast it froze my brain."

———•—•———

"PlayStation."

———•—•———

"*The Real World.*"

———•—•———

"I've had way too much Ritalin."

———•—•———

"My book bag is so heavy,
it's causing brain damage."

———•—•———

"I have this nagging dodge-ball injury."

"I get beat up a lot on the way to school."

———•·•———

"Society is letting me down."

———•·•———

"I'm just so tired from playing midnight basketball."

———•·•———

Vanishing Cash

"I had to pay protection to the lunchroom mafia again."

———•·•———

"I ate the money, of course. Wasn't it for lunch?"

———•·•———

"I put it in the market and lost big on Enron."

"Have you seen what they serve us?
Why waste money on that crap?"

———•—•———

"I gave it to a homeless guy on the way to school."

———•—•———

"In the spirit of Gandhi, I've been fasting for
twenty-one days. The money will go toward a
shrine at the school."

———•—•———

"Our math teacher made us pay for the lesson today."

———•—•———

"Boy, inflation is just killing this economy, isn't it?"

———•—•———

"I can buy food or books, but not both!"

"A five? Nope, you only gave me a dollar."

———•—•———

"I've been spending it on marijuana."

———•—•———

"I'm saving up for a tattoo."

———•—•———

"If I don't start saving now,
my retirement will not look so good."

———•—•———

"They should be paying me to eat that food!"

The Evaluation Season

"The school decided to save paper
and skip report cards this semester.
It's an environmental thing."

———•◦•———

"I didn't want to see it.
I assumed nobody else would want to either."

———•◦•———

"I needed time to hire an attorney
and prepare my defense."

———•◦•———

"Don't you think grading students
just destroys self-esteem?"

———•◦•———

"Wait until Friday.
I will have hacked into the system by then."

"Computer virus. Everything was lost."

———•••———

"Didn't I tell you about the fire?"

———•••———

"Not with capital punishment legal again."

———•••———

"It's the same as last time. Nothing new."

———•••———

"I was so busy studying that I forgot to show it to you."

———•••———

"I'm going to be an actor anyway."

———•••———

"The school district switched to a system with no grades."

"Einstein dropped out of school, and did it hurt him?"

———•◦•———

"I'm an artist. Report cards are but a canvas to me."

———•◦•———

Notes from Home

Each of these excuses was actually submitted to a school administrator by either a parent or a mischievous student. You'll need to modify them to suit your own child, of course.

"My son is under a doctor's care and should not take P. E. today. Please execute him."

———•◦•———

"Irving was absent yesterday because he missed his bust."

———•◦•———

"Please excuse Lisa for being absent. She was sick and I had her shot."

"My daughter was absent yesterday because she was tired. She spent a weekend with the Marines."

"Please excuse Gloria from gym today. She is administrating."

"Sallie won't be in school a week from Friday. We have to attend her funeral."

"Please excuse Jason for being absent yesterday. He had a cold and could not breed well."

"Please excuse Jennifer for missing school yesterday. We forgot to get the Sunday paper off the porch, and when we found it on Monday, we thought it was Sunday."

"Please excuse Mary for being absent yesterday.
She was in bed with gramps."

———•◦•———

"You'll have to excuse Steven from school tomorrow.
I'm psychic and he is going to be sick."

———•◦•———

"Megan could not come to school today because
she has been bothered by very close veins."

———•◦•———

"John has been absent because he had two teeth
taken out of his face."

———•◦•———

"Please excuse Ray Friday from school.
He has very loose vowels."

"Carlos was absent yesterday because he was playing football. He was hurt in the growing part."

———•·•———

"Please excuse Tommy for being absent yesterday. He had diarrhea and his boots leak."

———•·•———

"Please excuse Jimmy for being. It was his father's fault."

———•·•———

"I kept Billie home because she had to go Christmas shopping because I don't know what size she wears."

———•·•———

"I was here, but I was invisible."

———•·•———

"Please excuse Roland from P. E. for a few days. Yesterday he fell out of a tree and misplaced his hip."

For the Legally Unfortunate

"My car doesn't even go that fast!"

While it is not always a grand idea to make funnies when involved in the legal labyrinth, sometimes a well-placed excuse is your best friend. But this is a personal decision. If you want to make excuses, do so at your peril. The functionaries in the legal system have heard every—every—possible ploy. After all, everyone in prison is innocent, don't you know?

Red Lights in the Rearview

"You didn't want to race? My mistake."

"The more laws, the more offenders."

"Look at this chip in my windshield!
I'm going to catch the bastard who caused it."

"I was seeing how long that bug on
the windshield could hold on."

———•—•———

"My wife was doing her hair
and sprayed hairspray in my eye."

———•—•———

"I can't read the speedometer without my glasses."

———•—•———

"The speedometer must be busted."

———•—•———

"My contact lens fell into my Big Gulp."

———•—•———

"I haven't had a birthday in fourteen years,
so my license cannot be expired."

"I was trying to blow a leaf off my windshield." —

———•◦•———

"The speedometer must be busted."

———•◦•———

"I couldn't let my wife find beer
cans in the car."

———•◦•———

"I'm completely lost. Can you tell me
how to get to Interstate 80?"

———•◦•———

"I was lighting my crack pipe
and my gun fell off my lap and
got wedged against the gas pedal."

"I just got my brakes fixed.
I don't want to wear them out by stopping at lights."

———•◦•———

"I'm so drunk, I want to get home quickly
before I have an accident."

———•◦•———

"I don't even have a driver's license.
Why do I have to obey traffic laws?"

———•◦•———

"The batteries in your radar gun are dead."

———•◦•———

"I just got fired and I'm a little upset."

"I'm going to miss *Desperate Housewives*,
and it will be all your fault!"

———•◦•———

"I was feeling a bit of road rage. I'm fine now."

———•◦•———

"I was going downhill."

———•◦•———

"I've got to get this medicine to my grandmother.
She could have a seizure any minute!"

———•◦•———

"I just pulled out of the car wash.
I was trying to blow-dry the car."

"I was going way too fast to read the speed-limit signs."

———•◦•———

"There's no speed limit in my home state, Montana."

———•◦•———

"I was trying to hurry to a gas station
before I ran out completely!"

———•◦•———

"That doesn't mean kilometers per hour?"

———•◦•———

"My car has a mind of its own."

———•◦•———

"My 'check engine' light suddenly
came on—I thought the engine would blow up."

"I thought you were after someone else,
so I sped up to get out of your way."

————•◦•————

"When did they put up that stop sign?"

————•◦•————

"This isn't my car."

————•◦•————

"It looked green to me."

————•◦•————

"It's the only way I can meet police officers."

————•◦•————

"I just found out my girlfriend is pregnant."

"That's the speed limit? I thought it was the number of the highway."

———•◦•———

"Didn't you see that UFO behind me? You might be an alien, for all I know!"

———•◦•———

"I was just keeping up with the rest of the traffic!"

———•◦•———

"I'm on my way to the hospital to have the lead removed from my foot."

———•◦•———

"These videos are due back in fifteen minutes."

———•◦•———

"I'm from California. That was a California stop."

"The Viagra kicked in and I want to get
home and take advantage of it."

———•◆•———

"I've got to get home before the pizza guy shows up."

———•◆•———

"This car runs so well that seventy miles per hour
really only feels like forty."

———•◆•———

"We're out of diapers, and this car is only days old."

———•◆•———

"I had a vasectomy today and I really need
to get this prescription filled."

———•◆•———

"Damned cruise control! It malfunctions all the time."

"She kept saying, 'Hurry, hurry—the show is starting!'
Why don't you give her the ticket?"

———•◦•———

"We just went to a Schwarzenegger movie—we must still
be under the influence."

———•◦•———

"I just had surgery on my testicles and I need
to get some ice on them."

———•◦•———

"I just got my nipples pierced.
This seat belt is really killing me!"

———•◦•———

"I've got terrible diarrhea, so if you're
going to write a ticket, do it fast."

"Sorry, Officer, but I need to get to
the daycare center. My kid . . .

. . . has a raging fever, and because of liability,
they want her out now."

. . . had a seizure. It's over now,
but I'm scared and so is he."

. . . fell off the jungle gym and banged her head."

. . . fell down the steps and broke a tooth.
There's a lot of blood."

. . . got in a fight and spat on another kid.
I'm really embarrassed about this."

. . . has been evacuated. Someone smelled
gas in the building."

———————

"I'm thirty minutes late to my grandmother's funeral,
and I'm delivering the eulogy!"

"I'm studying to be a cop. I just wanted
to see how you approached the car."

———◆———

"My girlfriend's about to leave America forever,
and I have to get to the airport to stop her!"

———◆———

Should You Even Bother?

Inspired by *Speeding Excuses That Work*, by Alex Carroll

Before hitting up a police officer with an excuse,
exercise a little wisdom. Weigh these factors and decide
whether an excuse is appropriate before you make matters
worse for yourself.

1. *Are you guilty?* Cops make mistakes, and perhaps the
   one who pulled you over just misjudged. In this case,
   you don't need an excuse—the truth is your defense.
   With respect, tell the officer that you disagree with his
   assessment, but know when to quit arguing. You can
   always go to court and continue the fight there, and a
   judge may be more sympathetic and understanding than
   the cop, if the case ever gets that far.

2. *Will you fight the ticket?* Are you willing to go to court? Is it worth it to you to take time off work, drive to the courthouse, sit and wait, and get even more emotionally involved? If not, you have one shot at avoiding the ticket, and that is to convince the police officer not to give it to you. Use a good excuse, make your performance believable and memorable, or you'll just end up going home and writing a check.

3. *Where is the officer's ticket book? Is it visible?* If he doesn't have it handy, perhaps he wants to feel you out or point out that one of your taillights is not working. Don't jump in and say, "I'm so sorry I was speeding!" Give him a chance to speak, followed by a plausible excuse. Create for him the calm and peace he needs.

4. *Where are you?* If you're hours from home, you don't want to come back to fight the ticket. Again, the excuse is your only shot at getting out of it. If that doesn't work, you'll just have to pay the damned thing to avoid making a long return trip.

5. *Do you have a good excuse?* Okay, if you were the officer and someone gave you an obviously false and lame excuse for speeding, would you be more or less inclined to give the ticket? Yeah, I thought so. Evaluate the acceptability of your excuse and your ability to sell it before you let it fly. Otherwise, you might just piss somebody off.

6. *What's his rank?* As a general rule, the higher the rank of the officer, the less likely he or she is to give you a ticket. Quite simply, senior officers have better things to do than spend days in traffic court, so this little observation may help you in deciding what to do as boots clomp across asphalt, approaching your window.

7. *Is the officer wearing sunglasses? Why the hell is this relevant?* Police officers don't wear shades just to block out the sun. What they want to avoid is eye contact, connection, and empathy for the plight of the hapless (or helpless) driver. Should you still try to create an excuse? Consider the other factors in the list when deciding.

8. *What is the mood of the officer?* Some police officers just don't have a sense of humor when it comes to their jobs, and some don't want to acquire one. If you're stuck with a humorless law enforcer, perhaps better to get the whole affair over with and move on.

Four Wheels and the Fairer Sex

"I'm on my way to the beach. Care to join me?"

———•◦•———

"You know us girls aren't very good drivers."

———•◦•———

"I tripped over the cat and I think I broke one of my breast implants."

———•◦•———

"My lover's wife just left. I'm in a hurry to get over there."

"This is the first time my husband's
let me drive by myself."

"I'm ovulating and my husband's
fifteen minutes into Viagra time."

"Yeah, I know how fast I was going,
but with these cramps and the bloating,
I couldn't give a shit."

"Who knew Valium and iced tea would cause a reaction?"

"I just found out I'm pregnant.
I was trying to figure out who the father is."

"This damned mirror is too far away
for me to put on makeup while I drive."

———•◆•———

"Yeah, so I was speeding. So what?
You're probably cheating on your wife
just like he is on me. Aren't you?
Well, aren't you?"

———•◆•———

"Arrest me. I've seen so many women's
prison movies I'm eager to try it."

———•◆•———

"I'm sorry, but it's that time of the month
and I'm completely out of tampons."

———•◆•———

"This song makes me cry every time I hear it."

"I know I left the curling iron plugged in.
I've got to get home fast."

———•◦•———

"Look at my ring! It's a real diamond!
We'll have a spring wedding."

———•◦•———

"I can only dry my hair completely if I go really fast."

———•◦•———

"It must be the post-partum depression."

———•◦•———

"I have only one eye. What do you want me to watch,
the speedometer or the road?"

—*Moshe Dayan, Israeli politician,*
when pulled over for speeding by a police officer

You're More Likely to Get Pulled Over if . . .

Inspired by *Speeding Excuses That Work*, by Alex Carroll

Of course, our job is to help you make excuses . . . but what the hell, as a public service we'll throw in some info on avoiding having to make one.

1. *You drive in the fast lane.* Duh. Where are the vehicles that are going the fastest on the freeway? Well, it is called the fast lane. If the police tend to watch one lane over the others, which one do you think it would be?

2. *You change lanes a lot.* To police, this suggests that you are aggressive and reckless, and that you are more likely to cause an accident. Choose your lane, use your lane, love your lane—it will be good to you in the end.

3. *You drive a flashy car.* You know what salaries are like for public servants, so don't go flaunting your red Ferrari by driving it thirty miles per hour over the speed limit. You might as well just compound the idiocy by putting a sign on the side reading, "O. J. was framed!"

4. *You have a radar detector.* Police can see your radar detector. It's their job to enforce the law and ticket people when necessary, so of course they are going to be a tad resentful of folks who try actively to skirt the regulations. It's hard to fault police for not being particularly kind to those who try to make their jobs harder through technology.

5. *It's the beginning or end of the month.* According to some, the fabled quota system is alive and well. Reportedly, more tickets are given during the day and at the first and last parts of every month. Factor that into your plans of when to travel and at what speed.

6. *You don't wear a seat belt.* Many states have mandatory seat belt laws now, which means you can get pulled over just for not wearing one. In other situations, your ticket could include a penalty for not wearing a seat belt, even if that is not why you got pulled over. Yes, you may be a libertarian who thinks we have the right to live recklessly, but you may also end up a libertarian who pays stiff traffic fines.

7. *You are young.* My God, no! Not driving while young . . . But who deliberately drives with reckless abandon, youngsters or old fogies? Are you currently enjoying your salad days? Good for you. But know that the police are aware of your undeveloped judgment even as they attempt to save you from yourself.

8. *You are male.* Another in the litany of injustices this world inflicts upon each of us in one way or another. All that testosterone racing, probably a stereo turned up loud enough to shatter glass . . . why not push it a little? Of course, chances are good the officer who approaches your car will be male, so perhaps he'll understand.

9. *There are stickers on your car.* Yes, you have an opinion and you have the right to express it, but don't be surprised when it pisses off somebody in power. Think about it. A cop sees your stickers, watches the car longer than usual to read the bumper stickers, you make a common but still illegal right turn without a signal . . . you see how it works.

10. *You are alone in the car.* This suggests terrible things about police, but there are some bad apples in every line of work. A car full of people is a car full of witnesses, and otherwise it is your word against his. You like those odds?

11. *You are alone on the road.* It's much harder to pick out one car in a group and pull that car over than to simply tag a lone driver on an isolated road.

12. *You have a red car.* If all the cars in a group are speeding, who does the officer pull over? That's right, the red car! Or the neon yellow one, or . . .

13. *You have attention-getters.* You know, little accoutrements like flashy rims, oversized tires, tiny tires, or bald tires . . . maybe the car is raised, maybe it's lowered, maybe it can do both. Doing what you want with your car is fine, it's even great, but don't be surprised when calling attention to yourself yields negative results.

That Sickening Crunch
(from Actual Accident Reports)

"Coming home, I drove into the wrong house and
collided with a tree I don't have."

———•—•———

"The other car collided with mine without
giving warning of its intentions."

———•—•———

"I pulled away from the side of the road, glanced at my
mother-in-law, and headed over the embankment."

———•—•———

"I thought my window was down,
but found it was up when I put my hand through it."

———•—•———

"I had been driving my car for forty years when I fell
asleep at the wheel and had my accident."

"Truck backed through my windshield
into my wife's face."

———•◦•———

"The guy was all over the road; had to swerve
a number of times before I hit him."

———•◦•———

"In an attempt to kill a fly, I drove into a telephone pole."

———•◦•———

"I had been shopping for plants all day and was on my way
home. As I reached an intersection, a hedge sprang up,
obscuring my vision. I did not see the other car."

———•◦•———

"Collided with a stationary truck coming the other way."

"I was on the way to the doctor's with rear-end trouble when my universal joint gave way, causing me to have an accident."

―――•◦•―――

"As I approached the intersection, a stop sign suddenly appeared in a place where no stop sign has ever appeared before. I was unable to stop in time to avoid an accident."

―――•◦•―――

"To avoid hitting the bumper of the car in front, I struck the pedestrian."

―――•◦•―――

"My car was legally parked when it backed into the other vehicle."

"A pedestrian hit me and went under my car."

———•◦•———

"An invisible car came out of nowhere,
struck my car, and vanished."

———•◦•———

"I told the police that I was not injured,
but on removing my hat, I found that
I had a skull fracture."

———•◦•———

"I was sure the old fellow would never
make it to the other side of the roadway
when I struck him."

———•◦•———

"The pedestrian had no idea which direction to go,
so I ran over him."

"I saw the slow-moving, sad-faced old gentleman as he bounced off my car."

"The indirect cause of this accident was a little guy in a small car with a big mouth."

"I was thrown from my car as it left the road. I was later found in a ditch by some stray cows."

"The telephone pole was approaching fast. I was attempting to swerve out of its way when it struck my front end."

"I was unable to stop in time and the car crashed into the other vehicle. The driver and passengers then left immediately for a vacation with injuries."

"That van was parked in a place that logic told me it wouldn't be."

—Romark, a well-known hypnotist, after he attempted to drive a car blindfolded through the English town of Ilford and crashed into a police van

Hoping for O. J. Justice

"This isn't my house? Sorry."

———•••———

"Oh, that gun! That's not mine!"

———•••———

"Society made me what I am."

———•••———

"No, I'm just bringing these things back."

———•••———

"I'm sure the insurance will cover it."

170

"We may be finding, in some blacks, when the choke hold is applied, the veins and arteries do not open as fast as they do in normal people."

—Daryl Gates, former Los Angeles chief of police, on why twelve African-Americans mysteriously died between 1975 and 1982 from choke holds applied by LAPD officers

---

"I think it's important to keep the police employed."

"I was just playing a joke."

"Goodness knows, the trunk is big enough. It's big enough for two."

—Frank Thompson, South African citizen, on why in 1969 he forced his black servant to ride around in the trunk of his car

"I'm Robin Hood."

———•◦•———

"I'm trying to demonstrate why everyone
should be armed."

———•◦•———

"I have criminal genes."

———•◦•———

"The stocking is for a rare skin condition."

———•◦•———

"Someone must have put my fingerprints there."

———•◦•———

"I thought I was in a 'community property' state."

"Plasma TV sets are expensive."

"Photographs aren't reliable."

"I want to make sure McGruff
the Crime Dog has a job."

"No one told me not to."

"I made a terrible mistake. I got caught up in
the excitement of the moment. I would never
intentionally endanger the lives of my children."

—*Michael Jackson, after he jokingly dangled his
infant son over the balcony of a Berlin hotel room*

"I was framed."

———•••———

"I needed the money to buy drugs."

———•••———

"This is really just a fraternity prank."

———•••———

"I'm Santa's alter ego."

———•••———

"I may have entered, but nothing got broken."

———•••———

"I didn't do that well on my SATs."

"I was born with one of those guilty faces."

———•◦•———

"I tried working, but it just took
too much of my time."

———•◦•———

"All my skills are in the criminal arts."

———•◦•———

"I was negatively influenced by Wile E. Coyote
and Road Runner."

———•◦•———

"It isn't really stealing when
a riot's going on."

The Best Defense: A Really Good (Medical) Excuse

Inspired by *The Abuse Excuse*, by Alan M. Dershowitz

The further our species delves into the makeup of the human psyche, the more we realize . . . well, just how messed up we can possibly be! While we may revel in knowing more about ourselves, we also unearth new grist for the courtroom mill: If something bad happened to you, it can be your defense for having done something awful. Are all these defenses silly and offensive? Not at all, and many are indicative of legitimate mental trauma. But they're not always used responsibly. See what you think. Are we plumbing the depths of our fragile selves or just creating new excuses for deranged minds?

Battered Persons Syndrome: A gender-correct expansion of the battered woman's syndrome, this condition refers to a history of abuse that gradually creates "learned helplessness" in the abused individual. Over time, the abused feels powerless to end the abuse constructively or leave and sometimes resorts to violence to end the cycle.

Black Rage: Described by the late William Kunstler, the concept of black rage stems from a book of the same name by William H. Grier and Price M. Cobbs. Over time, the argument goes, African-Americans constantly subjected to inequity and injustice become enraged, though they appear calm on the surface. For some, this anger can be a catalyst for violent acts. Kunstler was constructing this defense for Colin Ferguson, who in 1993 shot twenty-five people on the Long Island Rail Road, killing six. Ferguson, however, fired his attorneys, represented himself, and was found guilty and imprisoned.

Chronic Lateness Syndrome: In 1986, a school district employee successfully sued his employer after being fired for being late regularly. The explanation is that lateness stems from some sort of psychological problem as opposed to shiftlessness or poor upbringing.

Cultural Norms Defense: In the 1980s, a Japanese immigrant to California, Fumiko Kimura, tried to commit a ritual suicide called oyaku-shinju by walking into the Pacific ocean with her two children. While her suicide failed, her children both drowned, and she was subsequently charged with first-degree murder, which would not have been the charge against her for the same action taken in Japan. Eventually, the defendant pled guilty to voluntary manslaughter and served one year in jail.

------◆------

Distant Father Syndrome: As the author of Iron John, a book about relationships between fathers and sons, Robert Bly once said, "[W]hen the son does not see his father's workplace, or what he produces . . . demons move into that empty place—demons of destruction." No explanation of what demons are capable of causing is necessary.

------◆------

Drug Abuse Defense: Not much explanation required here—we could also call this one the "Dude, I Was So Drunk" defense. Should a person be held responsible for things he or she does under the influence, given that the person chose to be under the influence in the first place?

"Everybody Does It" Defense: Texas Senator Kay Bailey Hutchison, accused of asking public employees to do personal tasks for her while she was state treasurer, argued that Governor Ann Richards, who preceded Hutchison, did the same thing.

Failure to File Syndrome: A professor of psychiatry explains why some fail to file their taxes: "[An] overall inability to act in one's own interest, all while one is actively anxious about a clear and present danger." Does it works? Not likely, considering the excuses the IRS officially rejects, but it has yet to be used as a defense in a criminal tax case.

Fan Obsession Syndrome: Robert Bardo was obsessed with actor Rebecca Schaeffer and killed her in 1989. Testifying psychiatrist Park Elliot Dietz claimed Bardo had this syndrome—a condition caused by repeated exposure to and identification with a particular celebrity. Maybe it's real, but should it have affected his trial? The jury didn't think so; he was convicted of first-degree murder.

Football Widow Syndrome: In 1994, a Florida woman, obviously frustrated that her husband changed the channel to watch a Sunday-afternoon football game, shot him. Before the shooting, she was considered a football widow because her husband abandoned her for the pigskin every week. After the shooting she was just a regular widow with a Football Widow defense. The corollary to this particular condition is Super Bowl Sunday Syndrome, detailed below.

———•◦•———

Genetics Defense: This defense argues that genes predispose a person to certain behavior, usually violent or antisocial. Central to this defense is the known existence of an XYY genetic abnormality in some people. Studies have shown that the XYY pattern is common among inmates jailed for violent crimes, but courts haven't been too eager to permit this type of testimony in criminal cases.

———•◦•———

Gone with the Wind *Syndrome:* Sounds breezy, doesn't it? Well, it's not. Some men believe sex must be spontaneous and they must overcome the initial resistance of their female partners. Another word to describe this creepy so-called romantic behavior: rape.

Meek Mate Syndrome: Moosa Hanoukai, an Iranian Jew living in Los Angeles, had been emotionally and verbally abused by his wife for twenty-five years but his religion and culture precluded him from divorcing her. So, in 1994, he bludgeoned her to death with a pipe wrench. The jury found that Meek Mate Syndrome had influenced his choices and found him guilt of voluntary manslaughter instead of murder.

"The Minister Made Me Do It" Defense: Attorneys for Michael Griffin, who was on trial for killing abortion clinic doctor David Gunn in 1993, tried this defense in an attempt to show that Griffin had been driven nearly to a nervous breakdown by antiabortion rhetoric. Others, they argued, should share the blame for driving him to violent action. The jury didn't buy the argument and convicted him in less than three hours.

Nice Lady Syndrome: This syndrome describes women who are so conditioned to be more concerned about the feelings of others than their own that they remain in unhappy and sometimes abusive relationships because they privilege their partner's wishes.

The Pornography Defense: The best-known proponent of this defense was Ted Bundy, a serial killer put to death who claimed, before his execution, that pornography had driven him to rape and murder. While some advocate prosecution of pornographers for contributing to sexual crimes, the courts have not accepted use of pornography as a mitigating factor in these cases.

Premenstrual Stress (PMS) Syndrome Defense: This defense was used successfully by Virginia doctor Geraldine Richter. Ms. Richter was acquitted of drunk-driving charges when a gynecologist convinced the court that her behavior had been consistent with PMS.

Rock-and-Roll Defense: Just how bad is rock-and-roll? Supposedly, Eric Harris and Dylan Klebold were greatly influenced by music before the Columbine shootings occurred. And in 1986 two Nevada families sued the band Judas Priest after their sons attempted suicide (one succeeded) while listening to their music. The band won the civil suit.

Super Bowl Sunday Syndrome: Some women's groups claim that more violence is committed against women on Super Bowl Sunday than on any other day of the year. While news stories and studies have attempted to prove a connection between the annual sporting event and domestic abuse, the jury remains out on a demonstrated relationship.

———•◆•———

Superjock Syndrome: Remind you of anyone? The term was coined by Dr. Susan Forward, a therapist for Nicole Brown Simpson. According to Forward, superjocks get used to the power, prestige, and adoration that come with being a professional athlete and think they are all-powerful, above the law.

———•◆•———

Television Defense: When Ronny Zamora, a fifteen-year-old Florida youth, killed elderly Elinor Haggart in 1977, his attorney argued that violent television programming had inspired the behavior. Ironically, cameras rolled throughout the trial and recorded a guilty verdict and life sentence.

UFO Survivor Syndrome: It may sound absurd, but research by a Harvard professor has demonstrated that people who insist they were abducted by aliens share a number of symptoms. (Cue Twilight Zone music.) In fact, there seems to be no existing clinical explanation for the set of symptoms these supposed abductees share.

Unhappy Gay Sailor Syndrome: One would think this syndrome refers to U.S. Navy gays and lesbians who despair at not being able to express their sexuality. In truth, this syndrome refers to the unfounded identification of lesbian and gay sailors as a source of weakness within the navy. When a gun turret exploded aboard the USS Iowa in 1989, many sailors immediately blamed gay and lesbian colleagues for causing the blast.

Ripped from the Headlines!

Remember the infamous "Twinkie defense"? The phrase was an inaccurate reduction of the defense of Dan White, who killed San Francisco Mayor George Moscone and White's colleague Harvey Milk in 1979. When medical experts testified that White's diet, which changed from fastidiously healthful to junk food, signaled his deteriorating mental state, many assumed angrily that his soft sentence came as a result. While analysis has shown the Twinkie defense to be insignificant in his sentencing, the term is frequently used as evidence of our failing legal system. Countless seemingly senseless explanations have emerged in defense of criminals, some of which are described here. Keep them in mind—you might find yourself at the defendant's table one day!

"You must die! You must die!"

—*U.S. Congressman Daniel Sickles, Civil War veteran, February 27, 1859. Sickles shot and killed Phillip Barton Key, son of "Star Spangled Banner" composer Francis Scott Key, after Sickles observed the younger Key outside his home calling to his wife. Aware that Key and his wife were having an affair, Sickles fired on an unarmed Key. Sickles's primary defense: He became temporarily insane at the prospect of his wife's infidelity. He was acquitted in one of the earliest uses of the insanity defense.*

"I am from Hungary. We are descendants of Genghis Khan and Attila the Hun. We are Hungarian freedom fighters."

—*Actor Zsa Zsa Gabor, calling on her lineage to explain why, in 1990, she slapped a Beverly Hills police officer who ticketed her for having expired license plates.*

"She molested me. She was just too pushy."

—*Robert Chambers, Jr., a 6'4" 220-pound man, explaining in 1986 why he killed 5'8" 120-pound Jennifer Levin in the "preppie murder case."*

———•◆•———

"We killed our parents because we were afraid."

—*Erik Menendez, who, along with his brother Lyle, shot his parents to death in August 1989. The two claimed they had been verbally, physically, and sexually abused by their parents for years and believed their parents would kill them to hide the history of abuse. They're now serving life sentences without the possibility of parole.*

———•◆•———

"I was told that I should shoplift. The director said I should try it out."

—*Colleen Rainey, a security guard for Saks Fifth Avenue, testifying in the shoplifting trial of Winona Ryder and recalling what the actor said to her after being arrested.*

"Who's gonna argue with Isaac Newton?"

—*Morganna Roberts, baseball's "Kissing Bandit," accused of criminal trespassing, after her attorney argued that gravity, combined with the weight of her breasts, carried her over the railing and into the playing field.*

———•◆•———

"What we have is Lorena Bobbitt's life juxtaposed against John Wayne Bobbitt's penis. In her mind, it was his penis from which she could not escape. At the end of this case, you will come to one conclusion. And that is that a life is more valuable than a penis."

—*Defense Attorney Lisa B. Kemler, explaining to the jury Lorena Bobbitt had felt it necessary to sever Mr. Bobbitt's penis while he slept because she was finally fed up with years of physical, sexual, and psychological abuse.*

———•◆•———

"He strangled women to ease his suffering."

—*Defense attorney Martin Elfman, arguing that the defendant "sought refuge in the world of prostitutes" and then killed them because he believed his real mother had been a prostitute and had abandoned him.*

"To be perfectly honest, what I'm really thinking
about are dollar signs."

—*Tonya Harding, after winning the 1994 Women's Figure
Skating Championship. Her success may have resulted from the
withdrawal of favorite Nancy Kerrigan, who had been injured in
an attack. Harding was stripped of her title after it was revealed
that she had been involved in a plot to deliberately injure
Kerrigan.*

"I blame [women] for everything. Everything evil that's
happened in the world . . . somehow goes back to them."

—*David Berkowitz, the "Son of Sam" killer, demonstrating that
at least part of his rationale for killing six people and terrorizing
New York in 1976 and 1977 was his hatred of women.*

"I was feeling like I was worthless, and maybe the
root of it is a self-esteem issue. I felt like nothing,
and I felt if I shot him, I would become something,
which is not true at all."

—*Mark David Chapman, explaining at a parole hearing
why in 1980 he fatally shot John Lennon in front of
Lennon's home in New York.*

"Dear Jodie: There is a definite possibility that I will be killed in my attempt to get Reagan. It is for this very reason that I am writing you this letter now. As you well know by now, I love you very much."

—*John Hinckley, Jr., in a letter written to actor Jodie Foster, with whom he was obsessed, before attempting in 1981 to assassinate President Ronald Reagan.*

———◆◆◆———

"I was rejected by my [biological] mother."

—*Joel David Rifkin, a New York serial killer who murdered seventeen prostitutes between 1989 and 1993.*

———◆◆◆———

"[This is] the price I pay for my open personality."

—*Boris Becker, German tennis star, regarding a paternity suit. When first accused of fathering the child, Becker said the Russian mafia had planted a Russian model, posing as a waitress, in the London restaurant Nobu, where the woman performed oral sex on Becker in a closet and then saved his sperm for insemination. He later withdrew this theory.*

"It doesn't seem right. It's like he's being
punished for recovering."

—*Defense attorney Adele Walker, arguing on behalf of
Paul Cox, who killed a young couple while in a drunken
stupor on New Year's Day 1989. Walker pointed out that
Cox's crime remained unsolved for years until he attended
Alcoholics Anonymous and was forced to reveal his secret in
keeping with the tenets of the organization.*

————◆————

"Why can't you share your bed? The most loving thing to
do is to share your bed with someone. It's very charming.
It's very sweet. It's what the whole world should do."

—*Entertainer Michael Jackson, in a British documentary
on his life aired in 2004 only months prior to his being
arrested and charged with child molestation.*

"All I did was love Nicole. That's all I did was love her."

—Orenthal James (O. J.) Simpson, despondent and suicidal, in a conversation with police involved in the infamous white Bronco chase on June 17, 1994.

"What the U.S. government did at Waco and Ruby Ridge was dirty. And I gave dirty back to them at Oklahoma City."

—Timothy McVeigh, executed for the 1995 bombing of an Oklahoma City federal building which resulted in the deaths of 168 children and adults, explaining his desire for retribution against agents of the Federal Bureau of Investigation (FBI) and the Bureau of Alcohol, Tobacco, and Firearms (ATF).

For Those Ties That Bind and Gag

"So sorry. I was trapped under something heavy."

Not too excited to return Aunt Martha's call? Forgot to send Uncle Joe a Christmas card? Or do you live in fear you'll run into an old friend in the grocery store whom you've been avoiding? These excuses will get you off the hook, or at least leave your victim scratching their heads long enough for you to escape.

I Haven't Called Because . . .

"You haven't heard? I suffer from telephonobia."

"I lost your number when I washed my hands."

"My cell phone fell into the toilet."

"I don't really enjoy phone sex."

"Because then I'd have to listen to you."

———•◦•———

"My horoscope warned me against
communication today."

———•◦•———

"Some guy was using the phone booth to
change into tights and a cape."

———•◦•———

"I can't tell when you're lying
on the phone."

———•◦•———

"Those postal service ads really swayed me."

"I dialed the wrong number and
gave up in frustration."

———•••———

"I thought you'd be angry that I hadn't
called you in such a long time."

———•••———

"I forgot your name."

———•••———

"I couldn't get the phone out of my
pocket with handcuffs on."

———•••———

"Nobody on the street would
give me a quarter."

"I hate the way you say hello."

———•·•———

"Because they said they'd shoot me if I did."

———•·•———

"I sobered up."

———•·•———

"Duct tape."

———•·•———

"The FBI monitors all my calls—
I wanted to protect you."

———•·•———

"I was testing your devotion."

I Haven't Written Because . . .

"I would have written sooner, but I got a
Christmas tree ornament stuck in my pancreas,
and it kept winking on and off, and I was too
distracted to write letters."

—*E. B. White, explaining why he
hadn't corresponded with a friend*

———◆•◆———

"I'm waiting for the cost of stamps to come down."

———◆•◆———

"I guess the warden tore up all my letters."

———◆•◆———

"I refuse to use outdated technology."

———◆•◆———

"I don't write, I only dictate."

"I'm too afraid of postal workers to send a letter."

———•◆•———

"It's taking me a while to pound
wood pulp into paper."

———•◆•———

"Umm . . . I smashed my writing
hand in the refrigerator."

———•◆•———

"It will take a while to learn to
use the other hand."

———•◆•———

"Pointy things make me really nervous."

———•◆•———

"I had this idea you were blind."

"Are you receiving mail again?"

———•◦•———

"I'm afraid you'd critique my writing."

———•◦•———

"I'm saving up to afford the postage."

———•◦•———

"Your reviews of my last letter were
rather lukewarm."

———•◦•———

"They moved my post office and I can't find it."

———•◦•———

"I didn't have a pen."

"I've been working on communicating
telepathically instead."

———•—•———

"I've been trying to choose
just the right paper."

———•—•———

"I hit my head and lost the
ability to write."

———•—•———

"I had a traumatic paper-cut
experience as a child."

———•—•———

"I'm deathly afraid of lead poisoning."

I Haven't E-mailed Because . . .

"The debt collectors were here and I'm waiting
for my thumbs to heal."

"I thought you moved to a country
without Internet service."

"I don't trust messages I didn't write
with my own hand."

"Every time I start, I get distracted by Internet porn."

"It's better if the FBI doesn't know
that you know me."

"I spilled a glass of wine into the keyboard."

———•———

"We got a virus—now all I can do is play Internet poker."

———•———

"I forgot how to type."

———•———

"We've gone native—no electricity in the house."

———•———

"Hotmail refuses to send messages until we
apologize for loading Outlook."

———•———

"You keep using words in your messages
I don't understand."

"We have gremlins in our computer."

———•◦•———

"After too many pop-up ads, Bill tossed
the computer out the window."

———•◦•———

"I've been in emoticon-withdrawal therapy."

———•◦•———

"The cat buried the keyboard in litter."

———•◦•———

"Yahoo mail put us on probation—only two
messages a day."

———•◦•———

"I crushed my fingers so I would stop scratching."

"I joined an Internet monastery and took a
vow of virtual silence."

———•◆•———

"I got my right hand stuck in a bowling ball."

———•◆•———

"No Internet service in state penitentiaries."

———•◆•———

Children Also Make Fine Excuses

Most people expect your children's needs to come first,
and even the needs of your spouse and extended family.
Use your beloved child for material for excuses if you're
ever asked to do something even less palatable than nursing
Junior's stomach flu or attending your spouse's office party.

"We couldn't find a baby-sitter brave
enough to come over."

"Spencer climbed into bed with a candy bar
and a thousand ants."

———•◆•———

"Our son is introducing us to his imaginary friend."

———•◆•———

"Nathan has his first date tonight and
we need to tail him."

———•◆•———

"I have to meet with her teacher and the principal
about her head spinning around."

———•◆•———

"The therapist told her she's gifted, and now she
won't talk to the other kids."

"We should wait until we get rid of Johnny's head lice."

———•———

"Right now Frank is explaining to the kids how
Mommy's egg gets fertilized."

———•———

"My son was playing 'filling station.' I have ten gallons
of water in my gas tank."

———•———

"If I don't walk him to the classroom, he gets beat
up for his lunch money."

———•———

"The attorney is here and we're going over
Johnny's Christmas list."

"I guess we didn't explain sex very well.
She's been throwing up every morning."

———•◦•———

"He dropped a cell phone into my pocket.
The police are reading me my rights now."

———•◦•———

"He found the condoms, Playboys, and gun
in the nightstand. We're about to have
a very serious discussion."

———•◦•———

"Robert got into the medicine cabinet and ate
a whole box of Ex-Lax."

———•◦•———

"Steven's been acting strangely and we need
to search his room for drugs."

"Our baby-sitter is sick, and the backup ran away to live in an Israeli kibbutz. My wife suggested the girl across the street, but I know she smokes a lot of pot and her boyfriend rides a motorcycle. We're afraid they might steal the silver or have sex on the leather sofa."

———•◆•———

"She's going on her first date tonight, so Bob is loading the shotgun."

———•◆•———

"The hazmat team just arrived to go through Eric's room."

———•◆•———

"We're starting the kids on ancient Greek tonight."

———•◆•———

"We just got the fire put out, and you wouldn't believe the mess."

207

"Jack was teaching her to drive, and now they're
talking to the police."

"No idea how he got a penny so far up his nose,
but we have to get it out."

Don't Limit it to One Species

You may love your friends and relatives; you may even
want to maintain your relationships with them. But it
doesn't mean you have to show up to every birthday party
and reunion. If you've run out of creative excuses for your
loved ones, try the animal kingdom.

"I lost my pet boa constrictor.
Could you help me find him?"

"My fish drowned and I need to hold a proper funeral."

"The cat was trying to hit snooze and knocked
the clock off the nightstand."

———•◦•———

"We're taking the Chihuahua to the vet for
growth hormone shots."

———•◦•———

"My cat hid my car keys.
He gets lonesome when I'm gone."

———•◦•———

"Jim got stuck in the sycamore tree.
We had to send the cat up to get him."

———•◦•———

"I have to drown orphaned kittens.
Want to help?"

"We have to bury the gerbil
while the ground is still soft."

———•◆•———

"The poodle has a beauty appointment."

———•◆•———

"I have to catch my tortoise."

———•◆•———

"The hamster is armed and out of its cage.
We're afraid the cat'll get it."

———•◆•———

"My dog threw his back out."

———•◆•———

"I have ants. Lots of them."

"The dachshund has an appointment to be shortened."

———•••———

"I'm teaching my ferret to yodel."

———•••———

"Sorry, but I need to tickle my llama to keep it alive."

———•••———

"My cat is lonely and stressed out.
If I don't spend quality time with him he'll
keep poking me in the eye while I sleep."

———•••———

"My hamsters are having babies tonight."

———•••———

"I have to go outside and referee a catfight."

"Some seagulls just flew over.
I need to go home and change."

"I'm trying to get my kookaburra to sit
in the old gum tree."

"I have to exercise my gelding."

"I was in the park feeding Fritos to the squirrels
and one of the damned things bit me."

I'm having my alpaca spayed on Wednesday."

"Gremlins."

———•◆•———

"I've got to clear my backyard of toadstools
before the dog eats them."

———•◆•———

"The javelinas tipped over the
garbage cans again."

———•◆•———

"I need to stay home and calm the goose—she
overhead someone say 'foie gras.'"

———•◆•———

"My cat has tap lessons
on Friday nights."

"Not now, I have a . . .

"... herd of antelope!"

"... rumpus of baboons!"

"... colony of beavers!"

"... congregation of alligators!"

"... army of caterpillars!"

"... quiver of cobras!"

"... murder of crows!"

"... mob of emus!"

"... shoal of herring!"

"... bloat of hippos!"

"... coterie of prairie dogs!"

—•—

"My rhubarb is infested with mealy worms."

"Not until I get rid of this plague of locusts."

———•◆•———

"I think it's the chiggers."

———•◆•———

I Have to Go Now . . .
(Split-second Departures)

"But my dear fellow, this is too bad.
I am monopolizing you."

—*Robert Browning, trying to rid himself of*
an inane conversationalist at a social event

———•◆•———

"I need to get to bed early. I start astronaut training
in the morning."

———•◆•———

"I need to drink the blood of unsuspecting mortals."

215

"My freezer went out completely—if I don't act fast,
Fluffy will thaw out!"

———•———

"I think I left my pants hanging
over a chair—imagine the wrinkles!"

———•———

"It's Aphorism Awareness Month—I can't put
it off until tomorrow."

———•———

"I'm sure I left a fork sticking out of the toaster."

———•———

"You make me physically ill."

———•———

"I think it was that expired milk I drank."

"I feel a possession coming on—gotta find a priest."

———•◆•———

"The wind just called my name."

———•◆•———

"That call was to tell me that
my brother is on fire!"

———•◆•———

"Oh . . . that smell . . . "

———•◆•———

"The spirits in this room are
demanding that I leave."

———•◆•———

"I'm experiencing the opposite of attraction."

"I have this thing about using other people's bathrooms."

———•◦•———

"I'll become a werewolf in the next fifteen minutes."

———•◦•———

"I felt a tug at my heartstrings and
I need to find the plucker."

———•◦•———

"I know I left the cap off the toothpaste."

———•◦•———

"I've got to touch up my graffiti tonight."

———•◦•———

"I left my insulin in my other jeans."

"I think I have to change my underwear.
Poor potty training."

———•·•———

"I feel like I'm going to faint and want to
be home when it happens."

———•·•———

"I forgot about my scheduled appendectomy."

———•·•———

"I really have to pee."

———•·•———

I'm Hanging Up Now . . .

"Johnny just put the cat in the microwave."

"There's a policeman running across my lawn,
waving his gun!"

———•·•———

"My car is rolling down the driveway into the street."

———•·•———

"Did you hear that click? Your phone is tapped."

———•·•———

"You're testing the limits of my attention span."

———•·•———

"Jeopardy's on . . ."

———•·•———

"I'm on fire."

"It just hit me how boring you are."

———•·•———

"Bill wants this line to look at computer porn."

———•·•———

"Uh-oh, I smell something decomposing."

———•·•———

"Those Jehovah's Witnesses are at the door again."

———•·•———

"I need to get back to my nervous breakdown."

———•·•———

"The guard is making me hang up now
and get back to my cell."

For he Relationship Entangled

"I was in heat."

As if family and friends are not hard enough to deal with, we have to go and get ourselves involved romantically as well, thereby complicating an already impossible communication scenario by adding that great simplifier: sex. No wonder so many of us lose our minds and forget ourselves—not to mention where we were last weekend—when trying to navigate intimate relationships.

Pushing the Bounds of Decency

"It's not a flaw. It's a fetish."

"If I don't do it regularly, I get blurred vision."

"I was punch-drunk in love."

"I sometimes bite things when I get startled."

"I'm a very sexual person."

———•—•———

" . . . [I] regret extremely my inability to attend your
banquet. It is the baby's night out, and I must stay
at home with the nurse."

—*Ring Lardner*

———•—•———

"I don't think I was constructed to be monogamous.
I don't think it's the nature of any man to be
monogamous. Men are propelled by genetically
ordained impulses over which they have no
control to distribute their seed into as many
females as possible."

—*Marlon Brando*

———•—•———

"I ended up with too much testosterone."

"I guess I thought you'd find it sexy."

"I would go out with women my age,
but there are no women my age."

—*George Burns, explaining why he
dated younger women*

"I was overcome with passion."

"Actually, the little head does most of my thinking."

"I must have misread the manual."

"I think someone put Spanish fly in my cocktail!"

"I'm cute enough to get away with it."

———•—•———

A Good Book Is Just as Satisfying

"Not tonight. I need to rearrange my sock drawer."

———•—•———

"I can only do it by the book. Do you have a copy of the Kama Sutra?"

———•—•———

"I caught myself in my zipper. I'm still a little sore."

———•—•———

"Satin sheets give me a rash."

———•—•———

"Performance anxiety."

"My boyfriend never lets a third person into bed."

———•◦•———

"Not in the restaurant."

———•◦•———

"I have a headache."

———•◦•———

"I was in my cave."

———•◦•———

"My nails are wet."

———•◦•———

"I was thinking about the stock market."

"The people in the next room might hear us."

———•◆•———

"Why aren't you wearing that blond wig and
black thing I bought you?"

———•◆•———

"Waterbeds make me throw up."

———•◆•———

"I'm really messed up from too
many self-help books."

———•◆•———

"I can't have sex in my parents' house!"

———•◆•———

"Sex is overrated in a marriage."

"Oh . . . too much tequila. Get out of the way . . . "

———•—•—•———

"My wave must have crashed."

———•—•—•———

"I can't do it when the dog is watching."

———•—•—•———

"Every time I look at you, I see your brother Ted."

———•—•—•———

Spousal Excuses

The excuses here are not intended for your spouse. Instead, they are provided to inspire a multitude of excuses you can create simply by drawing on your spouse as prime excuse material.

"My wife's hot and I need to stay home and fan her."

"He had to stay home and wash his toupee."

———•◦•———

"I can't afford a private investigator.
I'll have to keep tabs on her myself."

———•◦•———

"She wants me to practice taking out the
garbage until I get it right."

———•◦•———

"I've got to keep an eye on the house—that guy
with the letters comes by every day."

———•◦•———

"On Saturdays we get out the loofah."

———•◦•———

"She wants me to help her work on pro wrestling moves."

"My wife was showering when I said good-bye.
It will take a while for my clothes to dry."

"We're weighing the costs and benefits of polygamy."

"She wants to review the prenuptial
agreement with me again."

"I'm making him practice reading a map
before our vacation."

"She's taking me to the florist to remind me where it is."

"He's got the unibrow—we need to do some plucking!"

"If I let my husband cook, the kids might
starve and the cat is in danger."

———•◆•———

"Last time I let him go shopping, we ate frozen
burritos every meal for a week."

———•◆•———

"We're trying to decide if this really is a blessed union."

———•◆•———

"She's explaining to me which of the
kids are actually mine."

———•◆•———

"The Viagra finally kicked in."

———•◆•———

"I need to help my wife cover the children in plastic."

It's Not What It Looks Like

"I wasn't kissing her. I was whispering in her mouth."

—*Chico Marx, brother of Harpo and Groucho,*
when caught by his wife when he
was kissing another woman

———•·•·•———

"She wooed me with her siren song."

———•·•·•———

"That didn't count as sex."

———•·•·•———

"Dating younger is good for my self-image."

———•·•·•———

"I'm involved in secret sexual counseling
I forgot to tell you about."

"He reminded me of you."

———•◦•———

"I have to do this for my religion."

———•◦•———

"It's not what you think."

———•◦•———

"She was just helping me apply cream to a nasty rash."

———•◦•———

"I read your self-help books and felt I
should care for my own self-image."

———•◦•———

"I was drunk."

"I know you said you didn't want to see other people.
I didn't think it applied to me."

———•◦•———

"There are a thousand things, not including sex, which
could have gone on, which fall well short of adultery. . . .
Let's assume that some of the allegations that Hillary
sometimes—not necessarily being into regular sex with
men—might be true. Let's assume that this is a guy
who has been sexually active for a long time and then
got it that as president . . . he'd have to shut himself down.
You would then expect a variety of things which would
be quasi-sexual in nature but which would fall short of
it . . . Phone sex might be one of them, fantasies might
be one of them . . . Those all could be real things without
actually committing adultery."

—*Dick Morris, Clinton advisor, trying to
explain his boss's behavior*

———•◦•———

"I haven't lied to you. I just didn't tell the truth."

"I had a lot of tension to get rid of."

"She's your sister! It's still in the family!"

"Eating is not cheating."

—*Arnold Schwarzenegger, when caught on the set of* Eraser *in the midst of performing oral sex on a woman in his trailer*

"It was all just a joke."

"It's the Internet—not a real person."

"I have a sexual addiction, and I need help."

"I fell on top of her—it was an accident, really."

———•◦•———

"A man of action can't wear jewelry; he'll get it snagged."

—*Geraldo Rivera, in an explanation he gave*
to his first three wives on why he never wore
his wedding ring when traveling

———•◦•———

"The Viagra kicked in and I couldn't find you."

———•◦•———

"It's really all about team unity at work."

———•◦•———

"It's just a bonus I give to all the employees."

———•◦•———

"Some people collect stamps, I . . . "

"I blame it on the influence of hip-hop."

———•◆•———

"I was trying to act more European."

———•◆•———

"God is in my head, but the devil is in my pants."

—*Jonathan Winters*

———•◆•———

"You're just hallucinating a naked woman in our bed."

———•◆•———

"It [the stain on the blue dress] could have
been spinach dip or something."

—*Monica Lewinsky, on the offending mark
that sullied her infamous dress*

"She doesn't mind when I use the spatula."

———•◆•———

"I'm just helping escort him into manhood."

———•◆•———

Late Again?

If you're cheating and you haven't been caught yet, you might consider these excuses for coming home late from work.

"The boss kept us late for a mandatory pedicure."

———•◆•———

"We all got the company logo tattooed on our asses."

———•◆•———

"The video store made me watch an educational film on late fees."

"I had to talk my cubicle mate off a
fourteenth-floor ledge."

———•◆•———

"I decided to stand in line for free cheese."

———•◆•———

"Free tickets to the Ice Capades."

———•◆•———

"I decided to stop off at the orphanage to cheer
up the kids again."

———•◆•———

"You know the shepherds move the herd every Tuesday."

———•◆•———

"I went to a porno theater by myself."

"I got into a debate with a homeless
guy about string theory."

———◆◆◆———

"I accidentally locked my pants in the
car when I got to work."

———◆◆◆———

"I had to clean all that porn off my
hard drive before I left."

———◆◆◆———

"One of the radio stations was holding a
Jell-O jump, so I had to stop."

———◆◆◆———

"There was a long line at the Turkish bath."

Calling It a Day

"She refused to trim her nose hair."

"When her mother moved in, that was the last straw!"

"I got tired of wearing wigs and shaving my chest."

"His best friend wasn't me, it was Jack Daniel's."

"My intelligence was threatening."

"He bought me a set of socket wrenches for Valentine's."

"I got tired of her hitting me."

———•—•———

"I found the love letters he wrote to Dick Cheney."

———•—•———

"He told me he was breeding horses. Turns out he was only betting on them."

———•—•———

"Yeah, I hit her, but I didn't hit her more than the average guy beats his wife."

—*Ike Turner, musician and former husband of Tina Turner, attempting to explain in 1985 the degree to which he had abused his former wife and singing partner*

———•—•———

"After she passed the bar exam, she insisted I call her 'counselor.'"

"He said he was in the numbers game. I thought
he meant he was an accountant."

———◆◆◆———

"I got tired of Kentucky Fried Chicken every night."

———◆◆◆———

"He starting hiring the baby-sitter to come
over and watch him."

———◆◆◆———

"Every morning I'd have to see him sober."

———◆◆◆———

"She told her family I wear women's underwear."

———◆◆◆———

"He resented it when I went back to work
at the massage parlor."

243

"The cops arrested her for soliciting."

———•·•———

"She wasn't a natural blond."

———•·•———

"She never learned English."

———•·•———

"He spent our life savings on a sex-change operation."

———•·•———

"A friend lent her a copy of *The Feminine Mystique*."

———•·•———

"He quit his job to become an actor."

"She became a Mormon."

———•———

"The counselor begged us to do it."

———•———

"It was cheaper than filing a joint return."

———•———

"He asked me to watch *Funny Lady*
one time too many."

———•———

"Mother didn't really like her."

———•———

"She refused to play Escaped Convict
and the Warden's Wife."

"He wouldn't give up plaid pants."

———•◆•———

"His Princess Diana fascination got a little creepy."

———•◆•———

"She just couldn't get into polygamy."

———•◆•———

"I didn't consider his moving to the deep
fryer as 'career advancement.'"

———•◆•———

"She wouldn't whip me."

———•◆•———

"He was going to be in maximum security for too long."

Courting Is Such Nasty Business

"I would love to, but there's a Lawrence Welk
marathon on tonight."

———•◦•———

"I'm washing my hair. Each one. One at a time."

———•◦•———

"I'm from Mars; you're from Venus."

———•◦•———

"I got engaged last weekend. Yes, again."

———•◦•———

"I already went out with you once."

———•◦•———

"I have to go to Mozambique to do some relief work."

"I feel like a sister to you."

———•———

"I never date outside my species."

———•———

"I have this policy of never dating
anyone with back hair."

———•———

"I would never violate Don't Date Primates Week."

———•———

"You're a Scorpio? My God, that could be a
disaster if we dated!"

———•———

"I really do have prior commitments."

"They're expecting me at the White House."

———

"I need to talk to my geraniums."

———

"That was last night. Where were you?"

———

"This is the worst period I've ever had."

———

"I have syphilis."

———

"I'm part of an experimental control group. I can only date people referred to me based on a psychological evaluation."

"It may have cleared up enough
for one, but not for two."

—*Richard Sheridan, eighteenth-century Irish
playwright, at a woman's suggestion that they
walk together once the rain had abated*

———————

"Because hell is still in liquid form."

———————

"I don't really like cockfights."

———————

"I'd love to see that one! But not with you."

———————

"Not until I get through the
next stage of my therapy."

"I think my wife is getting suspicious."

———•◦•———

"My ex-husband just got out of jail
and he might show up sometime tonight."

———•◦•———

"You'd be violating the restraining order."

———•◦•———

"I value my life too much to say yes."

———•◦•———

"My houseplant isn't housebroken.
I need to stay home and clean the carpet."

———•◦•———

"Not unless you start bathing daily."

For Whomever You Happen to Be

One of the truly great thing about living in a free country in the twenty-first century is we can be anybody we choose. Who are you? An environmentalist? A Trekkie? A nut bar? Good for you! Use it to your advantage.

The Mystics

"I haven't been one with Mother Earth lately."

———◆·◆·◆———

"I can't do anything until the Age of Aquarius gets going!"

———◆·◆·◆———

"As you can clearly see, I have a short in my aura today."

———◆·◆·◆———

"I'm too psychic to go to parties."

———◆·◆·◆———

"My aromatherapist won't see me!"

"Bad karma combined with rapid dogma."

———•—•—

"I was a psycho in a past life."

———•—•—

"My avatar got deported."

———•—•—

"Proof that chaos theory exists!"

———•—•—

"I keep expecting nirvana and never get it."

———•—•—

"I've got to call someone—I can't remember my mantra."

"I got up on the wrong side of a bed of nails."

"My definition of truth got
washed with my jeans."

"I'm not worth a damn
without daily meditation."

"In my previous life I was a shepherd."

"I'm suffering from infected chakras."

"I was hypnotized."

"You're hallucinating!"

———•◦•———

"Last night I dreamed of emeralds,
a sign of impending danger."

———•◦•———

"This is what happens when
I don't consult my astrologer!"

———•◦•———

"My biorhythms must be off."

———•◦•———

"I thought Reggie was my animal guide,
but he's just a dog."

———•◦•———

"The results of my biofeedback were inconclusive."

255

"I've been in altered state of consciousness since lunch."

———◆◆◆———

"I'm just not feeling like the Buddha today."

———◆◆◆———

"Some sinister force had come in and applied the other energy source and taken care of the information on the tape."

—*White House Chief of Staff Alexander Haig (under President Richard Nixon), offering a theory to Judge John Sirica as to how eighteen minutes were erased from the White House Watergate tapes*

———◆◆◆———

"I had to return my telepathy to the manufacturer."

———◆◆◆———

"Saturn's in Scorpio this month."

"I need to see my homeopath, but he's sick."

"I started worshipping a new god, but she's ignoring me."

"I think that woman on the Psychic Network lied to me."

"I'm channeling the spirit of Marie Antoinette.
Have you seen my head?"

"I brought my yin, but I left my yang in the rental car."

"The cleaning lady thought my crystals were
rock salt and threw them away."

"My wife made tea before I'd finished reading the leaves."

———•◦•———

"Lord Vishnu is really pissed at me."

———•◦•———

"I can't channel dolphins in a land-locked state!"

———•◦•———

"My roommate destroyed my John Tesh CD."

———•◦•———

"I'm still trying to recover from the succubous experience."

———•◦•———

"Four of the five elements are conspiring against me."

"My out-of-body experience hasn't ended yet."

"The national organization revoked our Wicca charter."

"My shaman was arrested for possession
of a controlled substance."

"I can't function without my guru."

"My Ouija board advised me not to."

"Since my psychic birth, this all seems pretty stupid."

"My spirit guide got lost at Wal-Mart."

———◆·◆·◆———

"Most people have cockroaches. I have the ghosts of English monarchs."

———◆·◆·◆———

Excuses of the Zodiac

Aries: I was bored. It was the same old thing. I thought you'd finish for me. I didn't think it through. I got ahead of myself. My enthusiasm overtook me. Mars was in the wrong house. I felt a little hyper. She wanted to settle down. I was emulating Hercules.

———◆·◆·◆———

Taurus: It looked too good to pass up. I thought I was getting a good deal. It makes me feel better. I just like nice things. He was moving too fast. I told her it was just sex. I had to visit my mom. I've been a little depressed. It's just so soothing.

Gemini: I didn't know that would happen. I wanted to see
how it worked. Who, me? I wanted the experience. I was
just thinking out loud. I was testing you. I had a headache.
She asked what I was thinking. He didn't call the next day.

Cancer: I was just following tradition. It just felt right to me.
My emotions told me to. I was feeling nostalgic. He needs
me. She could use the support right now. I needed time for
myself. He wouldn't get rid of her picture.

Leo: I was just faking it. It was so mundane. It was worth a
shot. Why not? Big risk equals big reward. I overshot the
mark. I'm exhausted. She wanted to settle down. He flirted
with too many women.

Virgo: It could have been better. I just wasn't satisfied. The
numbers didn't add up. It needed to be washed again. I
didn't have my medication. I caught something at work. He
was never very touchy. She never complimented me.

Libra: I didn't have enough information. It was total chaos. I
  haven't finished my analysis. Too irrational. I was stressed. It
  wasn't fair. I just feel like crap. He said it was him or the job.
  She wasn't directed enough.

Scorpio: It was stupid. They're complete idiots. I won't talk to
  him. I can't work with anyone else. It meant everything to
  me. I'm suffering from withdrawal. We were too intense. He
  was passive.

Sagittarius: Every day the same thing. There was no higher
  ideal. It was morally ambiguous. Missed me, missed me, now
  you gotta kiss me. I've never been there before. I have a
  virus. He was holding me back. She was starting to bore me.

Capricorn: But it pays well. It didn't seem prudent. I was
  being practical. I needed the stability. I'm not in a hurry.
  Haste makes waste. I need some antihistamines. She was
  too impulsive. He didn't have a plan for his life.

Aquarius: It was all the rage. It just felt right at the time. We went with the mood. Who cares? Rules are meant to be broken. I can't be a conformer. I just need someone to talk to. She was a bit rigid. He couldn't live with compulsion.

———•◦•———

Pisces: I was going with the flow. I was a victim of circumstance. I was chasing a dream. Society doesn't accept me. I'm subject to change at any moment. I was overcome with emotion. She laughed at me when I cried. He said I was too emotional.

———•◦•———

The Religion-Phobic

"I'd much rather be in my own bed when I fall asleep."

———•◦•———

"Since my body is actually a temple,
I just stayed home by myself."

"That place is just full of sinners."

———•◆•———

"Not until I stop smoking, drinking, cursing, and
sacrificing small animals."

———•◆•———

"The woman whom thou gavest to be with me,
she gave me of the tree, and I did eat."

—*Adam*

———•◆•———

"The serpent beguiled me, and I did eat."

—*Eve*

———•◆•———

"My cat talks to God and
then explains things to me."

"My moral compass malfunctioned."

———•◆•———

"This old bearded guy asked me to help him get together two of each animal."

———•◆•———

"My name is Judas."

———•◆•———

"It's against my beliefs."

———•◆•———

"I joined an online church."

———•◆•———

"I'm too busy practicing witchcraft and becoming a lesbian."

"We're not supposed to do anything on Sunday."

———•◦•———

"It's the only day I can practice my bagpipes
without annoying people."

———•◦•———

"God appeared to me and told me he doesn't exist."

———•◦•———

"I can't stand when the minister says 'Jesus rocks!'"

———•◦•———

"My mail-order faith hasn't arrived yet."

———•◦•———

"The wafers and wine just never fill me up."

"I haven't memorized my Bible yet."

"I'm waiting for the church
to put in a coffee bar."

"I need to practice more before I can
speak in tongues."

"I have a Catholic soul, but a Lutheran stomach!"

—*Erasmus, Dutch Renaissance scholar
and theologian, in response to being
unbraided for failing to observe Lent*

"I worship Touchdown Jesus and the
last-minute Hail Mary."

"It's the only day I have time to prune my bonsai."

———•·•·•———

"My Cerealogy Genealogy Society meeting
is at the same time as church."

———•·•·•———

"Having only one god to worship gets so stale."

———•·•·•———

"Every time the minister says 'sinner,' he points
to me as an example."

———•·•·•———

"I decided to start my own church."

———•·•·•———

"I can't get past my fear of crosses."

"They never let me have extra
wine when I ask."

———————•◆•———————

"I'm not a god! But I did play one on TV."

———————•◆•———————

"I feel like I've learned everything already."

———————•◆•———————

"I hate it when the minister uses
that dummy to preach."

———————•◆•———————

"You'll have to excuse me. I've been in
need of an exorcism lately."

———————•◆•———————

"I got sucked in by a cult."

269

"This is totally normal behavior
for a radical."

———◦———

"I woke up with a strange man in my bed."

———◦———

"That was my evil twin."

———◦———

"It's Friday the thirteenth."

———◦———

"It was Satan's will."

———◦———

"I was raised in a coven of witches."

"Zeus has spoken."

———•◦•———

"I'm a little dizzy—vampires were drinking my blood."

———•◦•———

"Somebody sprayed me with holy water."

———•◦•———

"I'm afraid the exorcism didn't take."

———•◦•———

The Lunatic Fringe

"I'm busy all week building a boat
and collecting two of every animal."

———•◦•———

"Because that's what the voices told me to do."

"I got my value system from Jerry Springer."

———•———

"Excuse me, have you seen my other personality?
Her name is Jane."

———•———

"Sometimes obsessive, sometimes
compulsive—you have to roll with it."

———•———

"Since I read the Kinsey report, I'm so sexually
aggressive I can't go out."

———•———

"I'm a closet claustrophobic—don't tell anyone."

———•———

"It was a plea for attention—you look like my mother."

"I had a blowout on the road less traveled."

———◆◆◆———

"I think it was my inner child pooping in his diaper."

———◆◆◆———

"I was exercising my right to free expression
through my middle finger."

———◆◆◆———

"I internalized too much soap-opera wisdom."

———◆◆◆———

"I was a puppet of fate
like Kermit the frog."

———◆◆◆———

"Because your perfectionism is just so intimidating."

"You can't be surprised when a porcupine
is a little prickly."

"Iconoclastic peer pressure made me do it."

"I was undermisrepresented."

"I was robbed of my self-esteem and they
haven't caught the guy yet."

"I'm still trying to get over Elvis dying."

"I'm still working through the blender
incident from my childhood."

"That runs counter to every belief my
guru told me I hold."

———•◦•———

"I'm high-strung. Like Roberto Benigni on coke."

———•◦•———

"I was involved in this Guatemalan lab experiment."

———•◦•———

"Some people have two left feet.
I have two left brains."

———•◦•———

"The avocados told me I shouldn't go."

———•◦•———

"I'm meeting with the elves that night."

"Three words: attention deficit dis—hey,
that cloud looks like a giraffe."

———◆———

"I've got penguins and Santa at my house—
evidently, I'm bipolar."

———◆———

"I would, but I'm sure the FBI put a computer chip
in my head."

———◆———

"I'm not leaving the house . . . they'll shoot me
as soon as I get out the front door."

———◆———

"My depressive cycle is in full swing."

———◆———

"I lost my bottle of Prozac, and I'm all out of Paxil."

"I've got to hide the body and clean up this mess."

———•◦•———

"I'm working through this traumatic scrambling experience I had as an egg."

———•◦•———

"I can't commit to that—I don't know which personality I'll be in then."

———•◦•———

"Call my therapist! Call my therapist! Call my therapist!"

———•◦•———

"I said that when I was a ceramic coffee cup."

———•◦•———

"I'm working as three volunteers for Stamp Out Schizophrenia Day."

"My many phobias include a fear of single middle-aged men named Richard."

⎯⎯•⎯•⎯⎯

"On Sunday I usually rest from the six days spent creating the earth."

⎯⎯•⎯•⎯⎯

"You cannot expect the king of England to do what you say!"

⎯⎯•⎯•⎯⎯

"I've got post-traumatic stress from a really bad movie."

⎯⎯•⎯•⎯⎯

"Let me get back to you when I decide on my gender."

⎯⎯•⎯•⎯⎯

"The gnomes—they did it."

"Only if we go to a blue restaurant that serves vegetarian food and has a waiter named Bob."

———•◦•———

"Temporary insanity."

———•◦•———

The Star Struck

"I was seduced by the dark side of the Force."

———•◦•———

"I get a little sick when we hit warp speed."

———•◦•———

"You made the mistake of thinking I was an intelligent life form."

"I got lost in a labyrinth."

"I left the mother ship to do repair work
and HAL wouldn't let me back in."

"Actually, I'm a replicant."

"Put it in the X-Files."

"I got stuck in the eighth dimension."

"I got the memo. But you didn't end it with
'live long and prosper.'"

"If I told you, your life might be in danger."

———•◦•———

"I didn't check with the mother ship."

———•◦•———

"There's an alien living inside me and
it was about to explode through my chest."

———•◦•———

"I beamed up without my brain."

———•◦•———

"You were talking to my clone."

———•◦•———

"I was born and raised in Area 51."

"I thought I was invisible."

———•◆•———

"When did we enter the Twilight Zone?"

———•◆•———

"My body was snatched by invaders."

———•◆•———

"I was afraid of messing with the Prime Directive."

———•◆•———

"I think my brain chemistry got messed up
when I went through that window in time."

———•◆•———

"You mean this isn't the holodeck?"

"I'm only an android."

———•·•———

"The Force was most definitely not with me."

———•·•———

"You relate to Picard, but I'm more of a Kirk person."

———•·•———

"Well, it worked when Spock tried it in
episode forty-nine."

———•·•———

"I'm having a close encounter of the brain-dead kind."

———•·•———

"I'm still waiting for confirmation of your
directive from the Intergalactic Council."

"I got sucked into a black hole."

———•◆•———

"As a cyborg, I'm not capable of
human emotions."

———•◆•———

"Lord Vader gave me different instructions."

———•◆•———

"I haven't been the same since I tried time travel."

———•◆•———

"I thought we were in the Matrix."

———•◆•———

"Once again, my superpowers fail me when
I need them most."

"This cerebral implant really makes my ears ring."

———•◦•———

"A mad scientist took my good brain
and left me with this one."

———•◦•———

The Arboreal Embracers

"I ingested too many petroleum-based products."

———•◦•———

"I've killed enough of the world's trees."

—*Stephen King, on one of his reasons
for considering retirement*

———•◦•———

"With these clouds, my solar panels are dying."

"With that hole in the ozone, my brain is fried."

———•—•———

"Maybe a solar-powered car in Seattle wasn't
such a good idea."

———•—•———

"I've eaten a lot of genetically modified foods lately."

———•—•———

"I'm obsessed with spotted owls."

———•—•———

"The EPA has determined that my house is
completely surrounded by wetlands."

———•—•———

"I was bottle-fed."

"I was raised near Three Mile Island."

———•◆•———

"I'm living with asbestos wallpaper."

———•◆•———

"That Lyme disease is really starting to
screw me up."

———•◆•———

"I suffer from dry rot."

———•◆•———

"I've been trying to conserve by drinking my bathwater."

———•◆•———

"The government put a nuclear waste
repository behind my house."

"I quit coffee and I'm searching for
alternative sources of energy."

———•◦•———

"My ecological balance is questionable."

———•◦•———

"Due to the drought, I've been drinking
nothing but gasoline. It's cheaper."

———•◦•———

"My brain is an endangered species."

———•◦•———

"I am actually a carbon sink."

———•◦•———

"I'm really concerned about the beaver."

"Too much fresh air has made my head swim."

———•—•———

"Global warming has me all freaked out."

———•—•———

"I have bark beetles."

———•—•———

"My brain has gone the way of the dodo."

———•—•———

"I recycled my brain and the one
I got back isn't as smart."

———•—•———

"My parents were downwinders."

"I used to go swimming in the Erie Canal."

"I have mineral tailings for breakfast every day!"

"I'm running entirely on coal.
I've just got to make the switch."

"I thought, if bears can live on nuts and berries . . . !"

"I work for the government as a toxic waste dump."

The Evolved Males (or Not)

"Literature cannot be the business of a woman's life, and it ought not to be. The more she is engaged in her proper duties, the less leisure she will have for it, even as her accomplishment and recreation. To those duties you have not yet been called, and when you are, you will be less eager for celebrity."

—*Robert Southey, writing to Charlotte Brontë in the 1830s*

————◆•◆————

"If combat means living in a ditch, females have biological problems staying in a ditch for thirty days because they get infections . . . . On the other hand, men are basically little piglets: you drop them in a ditch, they roll around in it—it doesn't matter, you know. These things are very real . . . males are biologically driven to go out and hunt giraffes."

—*Newt Gingrich, former speaker of the U.S. House of Representatives and primary architect of 1994's Republican Revolution and Contract with America*

"Sensible and responsible women do not want to vote. The relative positions to be assumed by men and women in the working out of our civilization were assigned long ago by a higher intelligence than ours."

—*President Grover Cleveland,*
1885–1889; 1893–1897

"Linda, because she is a lady, is afraid of math."

—*George Brown, Democratic candidate for the California Assembly, in response to the suggestion during a mid-1990s campaign by his female Republican opponent, Linda Wilde, that the federal Department of Education should be eliminated*

"Jeremiah plainly tells us that when the people of a nation are willing to accept the leadership of a woman, it is a sure sign of God's curse."

—*Everett Sileven, clergyman and 1986 candidate for governor of Nebraska*

"Would she [Loretta Sanchez] have won with the name Larry Stafford? Play that mental game and you get an idea of the free ride a woman gets."

—*Bob Dornan, former Republican representative from California, after losing his 1996 reelection bid to Loretta Sanchez*

———•◦•———

"You're talking about a housewife running for mayor who, to my way of thinking, cannot devote as much time as I have to the office. A real fine lady is devoted to her husband and children and the activities of the home."

—*Joe Dienhart, mayor of West Lafayette, Indiana, from 1971–1979, while campaigning*

———•◦•———

"Women are not going to understand throw weights or what is happening in Afghanistan or what is happening in human rights."

—*Donald Regan, chief of staff for Ronald Reagan, putting his spin in 1985 on why he felt women had very little to contribute to politics*

"[Women are] less equipped psychologically to stay the course in the brawling arenas of business, commerce, industry, and the professions."

—*Pat Buchanan, former Nixon speechwriter and 1992 Republican presidential candidate, writing in 1983 as a conservative columnist*

———•◦•———

"See what happens when you let men into the cabinet!"

—*Madeleine Albright, Bill Clinton's secretary of state (1997–2000), on two male White House colleagues comparing shopping notes*

The Public Servant

In Retail

"That's a feature, not a flaw."

"They just don't build these things like they used to!"

"It probably just doesn't like you."

"Because it's made by little hands
in a third-world country."

"These things can be very temperamental."

"The technical term is 'planned obsolescence.'"

———•—•—•———

"It broke because you didn't buy the
extended warranty."

———•—•—•———

"It's supposed to make that noise."

———•—•—•———

"Did you let your kids use it?"

———•—•—•———

"It was made in Taiwan."

———•—•—•———

"It's too technical to explain."

"I don't think I like the tone of your question."

"I'm not the person that handles bitching."

"I was just lying to make the sale when I said that."

"Sorry. We don't accept returns from people like you."

"Your performance expectations were way too high."

"This store is closing in two weeks,
so I think you're screwed."

"I'm sure you forged that receipt."

———•◦•———

"I'm sure we don't sell anything that ugly."

———•◦•———

"We only take returns on Friday from
one o'clock to one fifteen."

———•◦•———

In Restaurants

"I know it was fresh very recently."

———•◦•———

"We like to keep the health department on their toes."

———•◦•———

"There's just no accounting for taste, is there?"

"We're a little shorthanded tonight."

———•—•———

"It's not the food. It's your mouth."

———•—•———

"It's probably the atmosphere in here."

———•—•———

"This isn't my table."

———•—•———

"This doesn't get you out of
having to tip me."

———•—•———

"I don't cook it. I just bring it out."

"We've got a new chef!"

———•—•———

"It's moving because it's so fresh."

———•—•———

"Hair is nothing but protein."

———•—•———

"On the other hand, it probably
won't kill you."

———•—•———

"No one else has complained about that."

———•—•———

"We observed the five-second rule."

"We had to stop letting him
cook with wine."

———◆———

"It's an old family recipe."

———◆———

"Freshness is just so yesterday."

———◆———

"The chef got a deal on week-old salmon."

———◆———

"We invite people in off the street to cook."

———◆———

"You're not paying enough to
have it cooked correctly."

"I remember the tip you left last time you were here."

———•◦•———

"Give the guy a break! He can't see the
food he's cooking!"

———•◦•———

"We're pushing squirrel as an 'exotic' meat."

———•◦•———

"The chef enjoys mashing potatoes
with his bare feet."

———•◦•———

"I don't think we share the same
definition of 'spoiled.'"

———•◦•———

"It isn't burned, it's blackened."

"The grill leaves marks that just look
like tire tracks."

———•—

"The chef got sick, so Juan the
dishwasher took over."

———•—

In Medicine

"You're just not very good at healing."

———•—

"Instead of the Hippocratic Oath,
I took the Hippocratic Suggestion."

———•—

"My English wasn't so good in medical school."

"That's all your insurance would pay for."

"I couldn't afford a good medical school."

"The hospital buys really crappy equipment."

"I wanted a good story for a medical journal."

"I just figured you don't necessarily
need both of them."

"It worked when they did it on TV."

"Remember, they call it 'practice.'"

"Sorry. I was coming off a wild bender at the time."

"In my case, 'doctor' is honorary."

"Don't blame me! It was the leeches' fault."

"I'm trying to save my hands for piano."

"We were all wearing masks.
How do you know it was me?"

"I'm sorry. Sometimes I'm just all thumbs."

———•———

"It wasn't on the floor for more
than five seconds."

———•———

"Maybe playing catch with it was a bad idea."

———•———

"If I make you better, I'll never
hear from you again!"

———•———

"This isn't as easy as you might think!"

———•———

"I get nauseated whenever I see blood."

"You don't really need it all the much, anyway."

———•◆•———

"I didn't know what it was attached to."

———•◆•———

"These nurses have the greatest sense of humor."

———•◆•———

"You have a very unique illness."

———•◆•———

"Who knew blood was so slippery?"

———•◆•———

"The nurse was sick, so we had to
use Manuel, the janitor."

Success and Money

*"I'm the firstborn. My parents made all
their mistakes on me."*

Some people say they're afraid of failure; others say
they're afraid of success. Still others rely on neither of these
fears—they have much more original excuses for being
screw-ups.

My Goal Is to Screw Up

"I have a pathological fear of success."

———•◆•———

"I was looking for love."

———•◆•———

"I kissed asses, just all the wrong ones."

———•◆•———

"I was a day-care baby."

"Picasso wasn't famous until he was almost dead."

———•◦•———

"I got Barbie instead of G.I. Joe."

———•◦•———

"I had Barney as a role model."

———•◦•———

"I really needed job skills, but they didn't teach those in kindergarten."

———•◦•———

"I'm a product of public schools."

———•◦•———

"I ran into the glass ceiling."

"My parents locked me in the basement
until I was eighteen."

———•·•———

"Both my parents were postal workers."

———•·•———

"My parents programmed
me to be a failure."

———•·•———

"My success has been more
critical than commercial."

———•·•———

"I mistakenly learned the habits
of ineffective people."

"My parents never encouraged me."

———•◦•———

"I refused to sleep with my boss."

———•◦•———

"That attempt I made in the sixties to join the Black Panthers has cursed me for life."

———•◦•———

"The mob pushed me out of town."

———•◦•———

"I was a crack baby."

———•◦•———

"Affirmative action."

"My parents always favored my brother."

———•••———

"I had an overprotective mother."

———•••———

"I haven't had my coffee."

———•••———

"My permanent record really holds me back."

———•••———

"I was adopted by hillbillies."

———•••———

"I was born so handsome, no one
ever takes me seriously."

"My twelve-step program was short a couple of steps."

———•••———

"My father was an overbearing sort."

———•••———

"It was the booze."

———•••———

"My wife spent my personal fortune on furs,
jewelry, and plastic surgeons."

———•••———

"My husband lost our life savings at the track."

———•••———

"Just look at my face."

"My soul needed Valium, not chicken soup."

———◆•◆———

"My work was never
intended for the masses."

———◆•◆———

"IQ doesn't measure creativity."

———◆•◆———

"My real strength is
emotional intelligence."

———◆•◆———

Artists and Entertainers

Living life in the public eye does not afford participants a better sense of the real and the fake. After all, there are reputations to protect. Hence, the excuses posited by those in the glitterati are generally accepted with credulity only by the hosts of Entertainment Tonight.

"I was stuck in traffic."

—*Tom Waits, musician, actor, and noted mumbler
and dissembler, responding to a question about why
he let six years pass between recording albums*

———•◆•———

Down south where I come from, you don't
go 'round hittin' too many white keys."

—*Eubie Blake, jazz musician and son of former slaves,
on why so many of his compositions were written
in complicated sharp and flat keys*

———•◆•———

"What I do now is all me daddy's fault, because he bought
me a guitar as a boy for no apparent reason."

—*Rod Stewart, on why he ended up being a rock-and-roll star*

———•◆•———

"All I needed was, like, five hours of sleep."

—*Mariah Carey, on being hospitalized
ostensibly for "exhaustion"*

"Nah, it's too embarrassing when I go out there
and nobody screams."

—*Michael Nesmith, one of the Monkees, when
fellow band member Davy Jones tried to encourage him
to come out on the balcony of an English hotel
room and wave to screaming fans below*

⚊•◆•⚊

"We just wanted to live life the American way.
We wanted to be stars."

—*Rob Pilatus, half of the singing duo Milli Vanilli,
explaining in 1990 why he and partner Fab Morvan
didn't actually do the singing on their first recording*

⚊•◆•⚊

"I don't feel we did wrong in taking this great country
away from them. There were great numbers of people
who needed land, and the Indians were selfishly trying
to keep it for themselves."

—*John Wayne, actor who usually played a cowboy on film,
reflecting on the treatment of Native Americans*

"I couldn't do a show where I just sing songs dressed in normal clothes. Anybody can do that."

—*Alice Cooper, rock-and-roll musician*

———•·•———

"I haven't made my good film yet."

—*Farrah Fawcett-Majors, on her career*

———•·•———

"It's much too good for him. He did not know what to do with it."

—*George Frideric Handel, German composer, on why he borrowed music from contemporary Giovanni Maria Bononcini*

———•·•———

"I take an oath. I'll never pick up a card again. Unless, of course, I have guests who want to play. Or unless I am a guest in another man's house. Or whatever circumstances arise."

—*Ira Gershwin, musician and lyricist, after a night of poker, when luck was not with him*

"If you don't make a bet every day, how will you
know if you're on a winning streak?"

—*Joe E. Lewis, comedian and singer*

———•·•———

"A wretched innkeeper at Nogent to whom I owe one
hundred francs . . . threatens to sell Reggie's dressing-case,
my overcoat, and two suits if I don't pay him by Saturday.
He has been detaining things and now threatens a sale."

—*Oscar Wilde, pleading for money from a friend in 1898*

———•·•———

"I am so sorry about my excuse. I had forgotten I
had used Nogent before. It shows the utter collapse
of my imagination."

—*Oscar Wilde, after the friend pointed out that the innkeeper
story was well-used*

Money and Truth Rarely Meet

"I had to post grandma's bail again on Friday night."

"I put everything I had into Enron stock."

"I was swindled out of my money by a gang of unethical accountants!"

"My furniture was repossessed, and I kept my life savings in the mattress."

"I'm a sucker for televangelists."

"They installed a new craps table at the Gas'n'Go."

———•◆•———

"My Tic-Tac addiction has sucked up all my money."

———•◆•———

"I can't stop spending it on
hookers and booze."

———•◆•———

"My parents are billing me for the cost
of my education."

———•◆•———

"I don't want to ruin my collection of
dollar-bill origami."

———•◆•———

"I support a child in Zimbabwe."

"I'm in the midst of a very personal Great Depression."

"I gave everything I have to the
Free Martha Stewart campaign."

"I've switched to the barter system.
Will you take eggs instead?"

"I had to make a big down payment on sod."

"The fifty-percent interest rate on my
credit card is just killing me!"

"I invested everything in Israeli pork-belly futures."

"My compulsion is giving money
to the homeless."

———•—•—

"God told me to give all my money to charity."

———•—•—

"I got this fascinating e-mail from a man in Nigeria."

———•—•—

"In the utopian economy,
we won't need money."

———•—•—

"We actually prefer the wings."

———•—•—

"There is a very good reason
I'm such a cheapskate!"

"I used up all of my money to get in
on the ground floor of Amway."

———•••———

"I can drop my Timex from tall buildings
and it will still work."

———•••———

"I daresay he does. But then, you see,
he has got a rich father and I haven't."

—*Lord Rothschild, nineteenth-century member
of the British House of Lords, explaining to a
cabby why his son always gives better tips*

———•••———

"On my way over to pay you back,
I was mugged by a roving band of gypsies!"

———•••———

"Kids outgrow their clothes in sixty days anyway."

"I was raised by a pack of rabid accountants."

———•◆•———

"It'll be in the dollar theater next month."

———•◆•———

"We want to see America first."

———•◆•———

"The walking is good for us."

———•◆•———

"Hamburger Helper tastes great all by itself."

———•◆•———

"Money will just screw up the kids."

"The Gourmet Buffet is just as good."

———•◆•———

"Nobody coming to the party has good taste anyway."

———•◆•———

"Boxed wine is just as good as bottled."

———•◆•———

"He never refilled my water glass."

———•◆•———

"I enjoy reading by candlelight."

———•◆•———

"But with used dryer sheets, I get a fresh scent every time I blow my nose."

"I don't mind waiting for the water
to heat over the fire."

———•◦•———

"The plants thrive on used dishwater."

———•◦•———

"Why buy napkins when I'm wearing a shirt?"

———•◦•———

"These are fine until toilet paper
goes on sale again."

———•◦•———

"There's plenty of salt in the bottom of a
pretzel bag without buying more."

Filling the Public Coffers
(Actual Excuses Used for Not Filing Taxes)

"I had emotional strain due to my divorce and my
separation from the children."

[Gasman v. Comm., T.C. Memo, 1967-42.]

———•◦•———

"I meant to mail the return but I left it in my office
while away on a business trip."

[Gillespie v. Comm., T.C. Memo, 1976-269.]

———•◦•———

"I was a single mom working three jobs."

[Throop v. Comm., T.C. Memo, 1994-10.]

———•◦•———

"My friends lost and withheld my records."

[Regan v. Comm., T.C. Memo, 1987-512.]

"The Paperwork Reduction Act relieves Americans of
their duty to file tax returns."

[Aldrich v. Comm., T.C. Memo 1993-290.]

———◆•◆———

"I haven't committed a crime. What I did was fail
to comply with the law."

—*New York City Mayor David Dinkins,
explaining his trouble with paying taxes*

———◆•◆———

"Payment of the income tax is voluntary."

[Partos v. Comm., T.C. Memo, 1991-408.]

———◆•◆———

"The Internal Revenue Code does not apply outside
of the District of Columbia."

[Buske v. Comm., T.C. Memo, 1998-29.]

"The tax law is unenforceable because the symbol '$' used
to specify the taxes is undefined and ambiguous."

[Lowman v. Comm., v. Comm., T.C. Memo, 1997-574.]

"I suffered from alcoholism." (Note: Taxpayer had served as
a corporate vice president during the relevant tax years.)

[Gardner v. Comm., T.C. Memo, 1982-542.]

"[Paying taxes] was one of the things I was always going
to take care of, but sometimes I did not have all the
funds available or I did not have all the documents
and materials I needed."

—*David Dinkins, former mayor of New York*

"I refuse to file the tax return on the grounds that it
violates my Fifth Amendment rights."

[Reiff v. Comm., 77 T.C. 1169 (1981).]

"Imposing a tax on my wages makes me a slave,
which is unconstitutional."

*[Matter of Ricky Sinclair, Jr., New York State Division of Tax
Appeals, No. DTA 819595 (19 February 2004).]*

———•—•———

"I am exempt from the federal income tax because
I am an African-American."

[Avery-Carter v. Comm., T.C. Memo, 1993-598.]

———•—•———

"I relied upon my prior tax representatives
and they gave me bad advice."

—Martha Stewart

———•—•———

"I didn't file my tax returns because I was an illegal alien."
(The petitioner had earned close to a million dollars
while working as a physician during the five tax
years in question.)

[Zamora Quezada v. Comm., T.C. Memo, 1997-481.]

"We filed our tax return late because I am a C.P.A. and I was too busy preparing other people's tax returns to file my own tax return on time."

[Sklar v. Commissioner, T.C. Memo 2000-118.]

———•◦•———

"I filed my returns late because when I was on the outside, my parents' accountant did my taxes but now I'm in prison for killing my parents and the prosecution doctors diagnosed [sic] me with a mixed personality disorder, defense doctors, with a mental disorder."

[Matter of Oliver Petrovich, New York State Division of Tax Appeals, No. DTA 816544 (20 January 2000).]

———•◦•———

"Our accountant was in Oklahoma taking care of his dying mother."

[Arctic Alaska Fisheries Corp. v. State of Washington, Wash. State Bd. of Tax Appeals, Dkt No. 47832 (1995).]

"The harassment at work exacerbated my stress-related medical problems, which necessitated my going out on disability leave, which compounded my misdiagnosed and untreated learning disabilities and caused me to have no income so I couldn't pay my property taxes."

[Jenrette v. Tracy, Ohio Bd. of Tax Appeals, No. 97-M-1027 (17 July 1998).]

———•◦•———

"I was convicted and imprisoned for not filing my 1987, 1988, 1989, and 1990 federal income tax returns, and after my release from prison I had difficulty compiling my records, so I didn't file my 1993, 1994, and 1995 Oregon state income tax returns."

[Pinski v. Dept. of Revenue, 14 OTR 376, 1998 Ore. Tax LEXIS 45 (Oregon Tax Ct., No. TC 4237, 1998).]

———•◦•———

"The 538 cartons of unlawfully stamped cigarettes found in my apartment were not mine, but were being held there by my son for someone known as 'the Fat Man.'"

[Matter of Bi Lan Jiang, New York State Div. of Tax Appeals, Docket No. DTA 819340 (17 June 2004).]

"When I was audited by the IRS many years ago, the IRS agent told me that he had never seen a taxpayer as scrupulous and honest in his affairs as me, and that I would never have to file a tax return again."

[Patterson v. Harper, 1999 U.S. Dist. LEXIS 18571, 99-2 U.S. Tax Cas. (CCH) Para. 50,983 (Dist. Utah 1999).]

———•◦•———

"I didn't file my income tax returns for 1987 or 1988 because I was afraid that doing so would draw attention to the fact that I had not filed for 1986."

[In re: Application for Admission to the Bar (Stransky), 431 Mass. 678; 729 N.E.2d 1085 (2000).]

———•◦•———

"I went to a lonely road and prayed that I should become self-sufficient and be able to help others, and a short time later I received a $836,939.19 check upon my discharge from the army. I didn't report it on my tax return because I thought the check was a miraculous answer to my prayer instead of a government error." (His final U.S. Army paycheck should have been $183.69.)

[United States v. Irvin, 67 F.3d 670 (8th Cir. 1995).]

"Our bookkeeper, who suffered from clinical depression due to an abusive relationship, failed to make the employment tax withholding payments to the IRS and then doctored the books and intercepted all mail from the IRS to cover her omissions." (Note: This was after the company had rehired the same bookkeeper who had been canned a few years previously for pulling the same trick. The first time it happened, the IRS abated the penalties. The second time the penalties were sustained.)

[Mason Motors Co. v. United States, 8 F.Supp.2d 1177 (D. Minn. 1998).]

"Our 1927 income tax return was signed in February 1928, and before I left home for spring training, I told my wife to file the return, but she forgot to file it until May 17."

—*Baseball legend Rogers Hornsby*

"My wife refused to sign the joint tax returns which were prepared for us."

[In re: O'Hallaren, 64 Ill. 2d 426, 356 N.E.2d 520 (1976).]

"I shouldn't be liable for the tax assessed against me because the IRS omitted the apostrophe from my name."

[Edward T. O'Toole v. Commissioner, T.C. Memo, 2002-265.]

"Our church refuses to withhold employee employment taxes because we believe that it is a sin to accept the authority of secular worldly governments."

[United States v. Indianapolis Baptist Temple, 224 F.3d 627 (7th Cir. 2000).]

"I attribute my tax filing failures to my stupidity and to the fees I owed to my tax accountant at the time."

[Matter of Anonymous, Defense Office of Hearings & Appeals, ISCR Case No. 99-0563 (18 February 2000).]

"I was diagnosed by a psychiatrist as having a tax phobia." (Petitioner served as a corporate vice president during the tax years at issue.)

[Kemmerer v. Commissioner, T.C. Memo, 1993-394.]

"I do not put my wife's social security number on my tax return because it is my tax return, not my wife's return. I have the right to do this. . . . Get real! Money is money! It has nothing to do with my marital status—except I spend more! Don't tell me that's the way it is, I would be in the same situation if my wife did not work or only worked and earned a small amount. . . . So you can shove it up your . . . " (Petitioner also tried to claim deductions for his dogs.)

[Matter of Douglas C. Brodmerkel, New York State Div. of Tax Appeals, Docket No. DTA 818043 (6 December 2001).]

———•◦•———

"I diagnosed myself as suffering from a bipolar mental disease characterized by mania and depression, which caused me to engage in spending binges and illusions of grandeur, and to not file my tax returns. My mental state is influenced by the lunar cycle and I am most prone to personal eccentricities during full-moon phases." (Petitioner was not a physician, but a lawyer who represented clients before the tax court.)

[Zadan v. Commissioner, T.C. Memo, 1993-85.]

"I stopped filing my tax returns because every time I sent something to the IRS, it just got them more provoked and they would come after me."

[Matter of Anonymous, Defense Office of Hearings & Appeals, ISCR Case No. 99-0714 (26 July 2001).]

———•◦•———

"I did not file my tax returns or pay my tax returns because I am the Messiah and the Witness from Heaven. I bought this land three hundred years ago, and as the owner of America, I am required to collect taxes, not pay them. After Watergate, President Nixon gave the presidency to me rather than to then Vice President Ford, and the United States owes me for twenty years of presidency wages."

[Watts v. Commissioner, T.C. Memo 1995-196.]

———•◦•———

"I thought that I would only be fined if I were caught cheating on my taxes; I didn't know that I could go to jail for it!"

[People v. Leota L. Sevilla, 132 Ill.2d 113, 547 N.E.2d 117 (1988).]

"My parents were interned in camps during World War II because of their Japanese ancestry, and my failure to file a tax return or pay the tax for the years 1994 through 2000 was a result of my mental illness caused by failure of the United States government to acknowledge the wrongfulness of its violation of the constitutional and civil rights of Japanese-Americans during World War II."

[Ozaki v. Commissioner, T.C. Memo, 2003-213.]

"My claiming of extra exemptions and failure to file my tax returns was a radical stand in protest of my employer's corporate greed, safety issues on the job, and my employer's callous treatment of the workers, and also the actions of the federal agents at Ruby Ridge and Waco."

[Matter of Anonymous, Defense Office of Hearings & Appeals, ISCR Case No. 01-24356 (11 October 2003).]

"We did not file our income tax returns for the period in question because of laziness, and because we spent more money than we received from selling cocaine."

[Anonymous v. Collection Division, Utah State Tax Commission, Appeal Nos. 91-0427 & 91-0428 (17 March 1992).]

338

"I shouldn't have to pay income tax on my salary, because I am a judge."

[Malta Inland Revenue, Bd. of Special Commissioners, Case No. 3/52 (28 May 1953).]

———•·•———

"The decedent's estate should not be subject to California income taxes on the postmortem residual royalties from the films the decedent made in California during her lifetime because when the decedent died she lived in New York."

—*Appeal of the Estate of Marilyn Monroe*

———•·•———

"Filing tax returns is against my religious beliefs."

[Owens v. Comm., T.C. Memo, 1968-4.]

———•·•———

"I am Amish and not up on all the rules."

[Hershberger d/b/a E & S Sawmill v. Zaino, Ohio Board of Tax Appeals, No. 01-V-1162 (12 April 2002).]

Food and Dining

"Oh, I'm sure just one more won't hurt."

When you find your diet hasn't afforded you the words "delicious" or "I'm stuffed" in weeks, the costs of eating healthy may seem to outweigh the benefits. Other times you're faced with food your far-sighted aunt made that smells of socks, and a cost-benefit analysis won't help you.

To Eat . . .

"The commercial told me I can't eat just one."

———•◦•———

"I'm sure it's a holiday somewhere."

———•◦•———

"The French eat it, and look how long they live."

———•◦•———

"I inherited my overweight uncle's wardrobe and I need to fit into it."

340

"The ants will start to gather if I don't eat it."

———•—

"Calories only collect if you eat sitting down."

———•—

"I actually hold it in my cheeks like a squirrel."

———•—

"My next job is going to be sumo wrestling."

———•—

"I have an extra-long colon."

———•—

"I'm having my stomach stapled
next month."

"I have to get that taste out of my mouth."

———•—•—•———

"I'm going to start smoking again on Friday."

———•—•—•———

"I just joined a gym."

———•—•—•———

"People tell me I'm funnier when I'm fat."

———•—•—•———

"It doesn't matter what I eat as long as
I drink lots of water."

———•—•—•———

"What's a football game without pizza?"

"My doctor took me off the weight-loss pills.
He said I was addicted."

———•—•———

"If you eat something and no one sees you,
it has no calories."

———•—•———

"I didn't want to insult the hostess."

———•—•———

"I'm starting the Atkins diet tomorrow."

———•—•———

"I was born with the fat gene."

———•—•———

"The more candy I eat, the sweeter I get."

"Drinking a diet soda destroys the calories."

———•◦•———

"Food that is broken up has no fat."

———•◦•———

"I'm exactly where I should be for
someone of my build."

———•◦•———

"They took me off the sports desk and
made me the restaurant critic."

———•◦•———

"I needed to make room in the refrigerator."

———•◦•———

"I lost my calorie counter."

"There are no calories in foods you lick off knives and spoons."

"Potatoes are vegetables, so French fries . . . "

"Ice cream has so much calcium."

"Children in Bangladesh are starving!"

"If calories are units of heat, frozen food has no calories."

"I'm currently on the all-candy diet."

Or Not to Eat . . .

"One should eat to live, not live to eat."

———•◆•———

"Squash is a verb, not a food."

———•◆•———

"I don't think it's dead yet."

———•◆•———

"I want to keep the rest of my food down."

———•◆•———

"Actually, 'casserole' in French means 'slop.'"

———•◆•———

"I'm not vegetarian, and those are vegetables."

"Save it for Popeye. I'm sure he'll love it."

———•••———

"That would require more ketchup
than we have."

———•••———

"I can't eat anything that has a face."

———•••———

"But they're so cute!"

———•••———

"I'm on a hunger strike to show solidarity
with my oppressed brothers."

———•••———

"I tried to give some to the dog and even
he wouldn't eat it."

"I've seen how sausages are made."

———•◦•———

Chocolate—God's Gift to Food

Some would say chocolate is second only to addictive substances in inspiring a consumer's devotion. Others would say chocoholism is just another addiction. Regardless, chocolate lovers really love their chocolate. Is any excuse necessary beyond love and devotion?

"Chocolate is loaded with antioxidants."

———•◦•———

"The strawberries underneath it are really good for me."

———•◦•———

"It could be worse. I could favor heroin."

———•◦•———

"Because I really, really like it."

"I want to support the cocoa farmers instead
of the coca farmers in Colombia."

———•◦•———

"I'm kind of depressed and chocolate
is a mood enhancer."

———•◦•———

"It doesn't impair my ability to
operate heavy machinery."

———•◦•———

"When I quit, I weep uncontrollably
and faint often."

———•◦•———

"It's European chocolate.
I can't just pass it up."

"Chocolate is a vegetable."

———•—•———

"Unlike my last boyfriend, it always satisfies
me and I don't have to lie to it."

———•—•———

"Food used for medicinal purposes has no calories."

———•—•———

Fending Off Vegetarians

Yes, they're probably also communists and members of
the ACLU. And we don't trust them, damn it. They're
vegetarians—or, God help us, vegans—and we generally
blame their behavior on a lack of protein. Even so, we have
to stave them off when they start throwing barbs about the
twenty-four-ounce porterhouse you're eating.

"If God didn't want us to eat baby cows, he
wouldn't have created Marsala."

"They don't feel a thing."

"If God didn't want us to eat beef, he
would have made cows smarter."

"God only cares whether we start to eat each other."

"If snails weren't meant to be eaten,
God would have made them faster."

"How can it be wrong when it tastes so good?"

"They're dumber than a stick and you know it."

"Charles Darwin. Survival of the fittest—
it's the way nature works."

———•◆•———

"I never had any pets as a child."

———•◆•———

"I have to have iron and protein in my diet."

———•◆•———

"Because I like it.
Now shut up and eat your tofu."

———•◆•———

"This is how our species has
survived for centuries."

Sport and Exercise

"When they pay me more, I'll start playing better!"

For those moments when you need an explanation for why you couldn't hit that little white ball, catch that game-winning pass, or make that clutch shot.

Running, Jumping, Catching, Hitting

"My jock was too small."

"We were bribed to throw it, obviously."

"I swallowed my tobacco."

"Two words: George Steinbrenner."

"I was thinking about endorsements."

———•·•———

"I must have had ambrosia."

—*Jim Gantner, former baseball player, on why he missed
a scheduled appearance on a talk-radio program*

———•·•———

"My talent won't fit on this court."

———•·•———

"Signing so many autographs gave me a nasty cramp."

———•·•———

"I wanted to make the pitcher look good for a change."

———•·•———

"Those other guys haven't won a game in a while."

"Instead of three warm-up swings, I only took two."

"I should have stayed with basketball."

"I didn't scratch my crotch for luck before the game."

"I started reading number 36's tattoos and it blew my concentration."

"Solar rays changed the flight of the ball."

"Someone stole my Gatorade."

"I lost it in the sun."

———•·•———

"His boss may have needed choking. It may
have been justified . . . someone should have asked the
question, 'What prompted that?'"

—*San Francisco Mayor Willie Brown,*
on why professional basketball player
Latrell Sprewell choked his coach

———•·•———

"Gawd, that guy I was guarding had horrible breath!"

———•·•———

"I guess I shouldn't have tried so hard to
impress those pro scouts."

———•·•———

"I'm still really depressed Michael Jordan retired."

"I thought I was ready to play, but it was just gas."

"They shouldn't permit geriatric umpires."

"I was afraid the fans would riot if we won."

"We're just playing for fun."

"I had a toothache during the first game. In the
second game I had a headache. In the third game
it was an attack of rheumatism. In the fourth game
I wasn't feeling well. And in the fifth game?
Well, must one have to win every game?"

—*Sawielly Tartakower, chess grand master,
explaining a series of dismal performances*

"It hasn't really been the same since the strike."

"I wasn't wearing my own socks."

"Just as the ball arrived, a drop
of sweat fell into my eye."

"Boy, those guys can really play!"

Game Excuses

Athletics are a source of colorful characters and
language, and we're not just talking about Casey Stengel
and Yogi Berra. There's a patter and lingo to sports that is
unique, and listening to athletes explained why they failed
or succeeded can be wildly entertaining.

"Bad luck."

—*Tommy Aaron, brother of career home-run record-holder Hank Aaron, on why he did not hit more home runs (13) in his professional career than his brother (753)*

"I had such a good jump on the pitcher that I just couldn't resist."

—*Lou Novikoff, Chicago Cubs outfielder, on why he tried to steal third base even though the bases were loaded*

"I missed my put for an eleven."

—*Arnold Palmer, golf champion, explaining how he managed to take twelve shots to sink the ball on a par-five hole*

"Honey, I just forgot to duck."

—*Jack Dempsey, world champion boxer, to his wife after he lost the heavyweight title to Gene Tunney on in 1926; Ronald Reagan recycled the memorable line after he was shot in a 1981 assassination attempt*

"This year I'm told the team did well because one pitcher had a fine curve ball. I understand that a curve ball is thrown with a deliberate attempt to deceive. Surely that is not an ability we should want to foster at Harvard."

—*Charles William Eliot, Harvard president from 1869 to 1909, on why he decided to reduce support for the baseball team despite its success*

———•◦•———

"What's everyone blaming me for? Blame Felix. I wouldn't have hit into the double plays if he hadn't hit singles."

—*Joe Torre, playing for the New York Mets in 1975, after, incredibly, hitting into four double plays in one game*

———•◦•———

"He said he missed one kick because the ball was too new. He said he missed another because the helmet was too tight. He missed another because the ball was upside down. We played a game at Canton and he said he missed because the grass was too high. The next week he missed another field goal. He said, 'Uncle Ben, the grass was too high.' I said, 'Rafael, we're playing on Astroturf.'"

—*Ben Agajanian, ex-NFL kicker and kicking coach, on the best excuses by Dallas Cowboy kicker Rafael Septien*

"Anyone can have an off decade."

—*Larry Cole, Dallas Cowboys defensive lineman, on why he went scoreless during the 1970s before returning a fumble for a touchdown in 1980*

"We have a great bunch of outside shooters. Unfortunately, all our games are played indoors."

—*Weldon Drew, New Mexico State basketball coach*

"I don't feel like I choked. It was either the wind, or the full moon, or the tides, or gravity, or something."

—*Kurt Dasbach, Columbia University kicker, on missing a thirty-six-yard field goal that would have ended the school's thirty-nine-game losing streak*

"I don't manage by the book because I've never met the guy who wrote it."

—*Dick Williams, manager of the Seattle Mariners*

"I had some bad gravity out there. It's gravity that makes the ball drop in the hole, right? Well, I was hitting the putts beautiful, but the ball wasn't dropping."

—*Harry Toscano, professional golfer,*
on a bad round he endured

———◆———

"Reggie, you're in Dodger country."

—*Phil McHone, California Highway Patrol officer, explaining in*
1974 to Oakland A's star Reggie Jackson why he had been
pulled over twice in twenty minutes driving down Interstate 5 in
southern California; Jackson had recently led the A's to a World
Series title over the Los Angeles Dodgers

———◆———

"It would have been different if I had eaten that thing because we were losing or because of disrespect. I ate it because I was hungry."

—*Ezra Johnson, Green Bay Packers football player,*
after he was fined a thousand dollars for eating
a hot dog during a 38–0 preseason loss

"When I took this job, I promised our fans I'd show them a Rose Bowl team."

—Lee Corso, Indiana University football coach, on why he included the University of Southern California Trojans on his team's schedule

———•◆•———

"It was the power, the chocolate thunder. I could feel it surging through my body, fighting to get out. I had no control over it."

—Darryl Dawkins, Philadelphia 76ers basketball player, after shattering a backboard on a slam dunk

———•◆•———

"Madame, I am trying to determine exactly how disgusting it is."

—Earl Strom, NBA referee, after an elderly woman approached to ask why he was watching a "disgusting" performance by four topless women promoting a local nightclub during a timeout at an Indiana Pacers game

"You can't beat the peace and quiet around a cemetery."

—*Richie Hebner, Philadelphia Phillies first baseman,*
on his off-season employment as a gravedigger

"We just need to work on some fundamentals."

—*Gilbert Alvarez, girls' basketball coach at North Dallas*
High School, after his team lost a game 136–7

"I have to be honest. I think I lost because
I wasn't wearing a bra."

—*Pam Teeguarden, professional tennis player, explaining that she*
felt the linespeople had been against her during the match

"I got tired, my ears started popping, the rubber came off
my tennis shoes, I got a cramp, and I lost one of my
contact lenses. Other than that, I was in great shape."

—*Bob Lutz, professional tennis player, after*
losing a game to Guillermo Vilas

"I clashed with the drapes."

—*Jake La Motta, middleweight boxing champion,
on why his first of six wives left him*

———◆———

"Night in and night out, we have to score ten field goals
more just to make it close. I blame the press. If we don't
get any respect here, why should we get it from the
officials?"

—*Butch Beard, New York Knicks assistant coach,
on the team's struggles*

———◆———

"I never set out to hurt anybody deliberately unless it was,
you know, important—like a league game or something."

—*Dick Butkus, Chicago Bears linebacker*

———◆———

"My sister's expecting a baby and I don't know if I'm
going to be an uncle or an aunt."

—*Chuck Nevitt, explaining to North Carolina State basketball
coach Jim Valvano why he seemed so nervous during practice*

"I do not participate in any sport with ambulances
at the bottom of a hill."

—*Erma Bombeck, syndicated columnist,
on why she did not ski*

———•◦•———

"I don't think any wife would stand for a husband
traveling around dressed like a chicken."

—*Ted Giannoulas, also known as the San Diego
Chicken, on why he never married*

———•◦•———

"Following the lead of NFL coaches who do not
play many of their starters, I don't use any of my
first-string verbs and adjectives."

—*Glen Sheeley, a sports writer in Atlanta, explaining
his coverage of preseason NFL football games*

"You can't do anything and you're eating grass
the whole time."

—*Mark McGwire, Oakland A's slugger, on why he
didn't like to get involved in baseball brawls,
particularly from the bottom of the pile*

"I don't have the average thirty-eight-year-old's body.
I know my face looks old, but if you'd slid
head-first for sixteen years, you'd be ugly too."

—*Pete Rose, Cincinnati Reds baseball legend,
on why he wasn't over the hill at thirty-eight*

"Because then there'd be two languages
I couldn't speak—French and English."

—*Casey Stengel, baseball player and, more notoriously,
manager, on why he never visited Montreal*

"Golf seemed a silly thing to do for a living."

—Willie Auchterlonie, on why he
retired after winning the British Open

"I couldn't pronounce it myself."

—Bob Miller, New York Mets pitcher, on why he
changed his last name from Gemeinweiser

"Any kid who would leave that wonderful
weather is too dumb to play for us."

—Alex Agase, Purdue University football coach, on why he did
not waste time recruiting players from California

"You were open."

—Bud Ogden, Philadelphia 76ers basketball player, on why he
threw a ball to a reporter sitting on press row during a game

"He came here when he heard A & M was an engineering school. But when he found out they wouldn't let him drive a train, he left."

—*Shelby Metcalf, Texas A & M University basketball coach, on why a player decided to leave school*

———————

"I cover up everything I can."

—*Joe Torre, then Atlanta Braves manager, on why he called his hairstyle a Watergate*

———————

"Well, I had such a good year, I didn't want to forget it."

—*Dick "Dr. Strangelove" Stuart, Boston Red Sox slugger, to a police officer who pulled him over in 1964 for still having 1963 license plates on his car*

———————

"Whoever stole it is spending less money than my wife."

—*Ilie Nastase, tennis pro, on why he didn't report his American Express card missing when it was stolen*

"Perhaps it is precisely because of our great wines
that we have not had great track teams."

—*Michel Lourie, coach for the French national track
team, on why the country had failed to produce track
stars the equivalent of the country's wine*

———◆———

"Howard's not going to like seeing this, but the reason is,
he doesn't look good in stretch pants."

—*Roone Arledge, ABC TV producer, on
why Howard Cosell was not included in 1984 Olympic coverage*

———◆———

"I was the only complete ass they had.
Here, I just fit right in."

—*Tug McGraw, Philadelphia Phillies relief pitcher, on why he
was traded from the New York Mets to the Phillies*

———◆———

"I already have two white guys on my team."

—*Cotton Fitzsimmons, coach of the Kansas City Kings, on why
he decided not to select Larry Bird in the 1978 NBA draft*

"I was taking a shower and found a pencil behind my ear. I have no idea how long it was there."

—*Bunky Henry, professional golfer, on why he finally cut his long hair*

———

"I just got tired of walking. That's a very large campus."

—*Bob McAdoo, professional basketball player, on why he decided to leave the University of North Carolina after his junior year*

———

"It was the closest thing to baseball I could find."

—*Syd O'Brien, former professional baseball player, on why he became a liquor distributor after retiring*

———

"I've never heard of a plane that backed into a mountain."

—*C. M. Newton, Vanderbilt University basketball coach, on why he always chose to sit in the back row of seats on a plane*

"I usually take my wife with me on trips because she's too ugly to kiss good-bye."

—*Bum Phillips, head coach of the New Orleans Saints*

———•—•———

"Prayer never seems to work for me on the golf course. I think it has something to do with my being a terrible putter."

—*Billy Graham, religious leader, on his golf game and God*

———•—•———

Whacking and Chasing Balls

I'm Scottish. It's in my blood."

———•—•———

"My ex-wife hates golf more than anything."

———•—•———

"I want to spend more quality time with friends."

372

"I'm addicted to spiky shoes and plaid pants."

———•••———

"The doctor recommended golf as therapy."

———•••———

"I need to see if all this meditation is helping my game."

———•••———

"On his death bed, my father insisted I spend the inheritance on green fees."

———•••———

"I need to work on my tan."

———•••———

"I'm sure I can get the cart over the creek this time."

"It's a requirement for the sales staff."

"I have to beat the hell out of something."

"Beer is half-price every Sunday."

"I ran out of gas in front of the course."

"It's the only place I can get a really good burger."

"It's not for me—my son needs the practice."

"My wife asked to me get lost for a while."

"With a name like Fuzzy Tiger, what did you expect?"

"It was either this or sex with my wife."

"The fishing isn't too good right now."

"The bowling alley was closed."

"The Bears didn't make the playoffs."

"I'm stocking up on free pencils for the office."

———•◆•———

"I need some lawn-care tips."

———•◆•———

"We're all out of beer at home."

———•◆•———

"The turbo-charged golf carts came in last week."

———•◆•———

"I want to test this laser eye surgery."

———•◆•———

"Wednesday is Frito-pie day at the clubhouse."

"I'm really an outdoorsman."

———•◦•———

"I have to get even with a gopher on the eighth hole."

———•◦•———

"I like to hit things."

———•◦•———

"I hear your scores really improve when you're sober."

———•◦•———

"I'm going to keep playing until I find the
lucky ball I lost last year."

———•◦•———

"My bat is in for repairs, so cricket is right out."

"My wife's sick—I think I can finally beat her."

———•◦•———

"The voices in my head told me to go golfing."

———•◦•———

"I want to test the effectiveness of my
anger management courses."

———•◦•———

"I love urinating in the great outdoors."

———•◦•———

"Really great hot dogs."

———•◦•———

"They added a new beer to the beverage cart."

"I just love screaming 'Fore!'"

Excuses for Poor Golfing

"Boy, do I have to pee!"

"Why do these geese keep following me?"

"My angle of impact exceeded the compression capabilities of the ball's core."

"Weight lifting has really thrown off my game."

"I saw my caddy put a curse on me."

"I know I look terrible in green jackets."

———•◦•———

"That ball must have too many dimples."

———•◦•———

"These balls are orange! I can only play with white balls."

———•◦•———

"My cell phone started vibrating during that shot."

———•◦•———

"Must be the beer."

———•◦•———

"I don't miss being a woman, but hitting from
the red tees was nice."

"My wife was awarded the lessons in the divorce."

———•—•———

"I haven't seen my guru in a week!"

———•—•———

"This riding-in-a-cart stuff is too cushy."

———•—•———

"My balls are dirty."

———•—•———

"I can only afford lessons over the Internet."

———•—•———

"Bad golf karma."

"I visualized a double-bogey."

* * *

"The prison didn't have a course."

* * *

"I keep thinking of that duck I accidentally killed."

* * *

"I know that tree is new."

* * *

"I bent my putter chasing raccoons out of the backyard."

* * *

"Usually, I'm so drunk by now,
they kick me off the course."

"I'm used to a completely different type of grass."

———•—•———

"I've got whiplash from the way you drive the cart."

———•—•———

"I can't see anything other than that shirt you're wearing."

———•—•———

"I play much better in Spanish than English."

———•—•———

"Sex is just killing my game—I may have to give it up."

———•—•———

"This is the heaviest air I've ever seen."

"My ball seems to have a drinking problem, too."

———•◦•———

"The beer-cart girl doesn't love me anymore."

———•◦•———

"It's not me! The green is spinning!"

———•◦•———

"There is goose shit everywhere!"

———•◦•———

"I can't make a put unless there's a ramp to climb
and a windmill in the way."

———•◦•———

"I just can't swing the same way since I took that bullet."

"I don't get the Golf Channel."

"Scuba diving has ruined my equilibrium."

"I don't play any better than my group,
and you guys suck."

"I can't play worth a damn without medication."

"I like playing with women. I'm motivated
by the fear of losing to them."

"This is the first time I've played with shoes."

"My ball's looking for a vacation—it keeps landing in the sand."

———•—•—

"These are rental clubs."

———•—•—

"I decided to give up sex yesterday."

———•—•—

"The restraining order has kept me away from the club for a while."

———•—•—

"I always blow the shot when there's money riding on it."

———•—•—

"Next time, I'll have to steal better clubs."

"I can't hit a shot unless there's some money involved."

———•◦•———

"My caddy was deported."

———•◦•———

"I need new glasses."

———•◦•———

"I get flashbacks of this ball-washing incident
from high school."

———•◦•———

"This jock itch is really messing with my stance!"

———•◦•———

"I'm just so afraid the ball is in great pain."

"I'm only here to get away from my wife."

———•·•———

"I forgot to 'be the ball.'"

———•·•———

The One That Got Away

If there's one pastime that lends itself more than others to excuses, it's fishing. Perhaps we can blame the vagaries and fluctuating successes and failures of this luxury for eliciting excuses, but rarely does anyone tell the bald-faced truth when it comes to stalking wily trout and returning with nothing.

"I was just teaching my worms to swim."

———•·•———

"My kids ate all the bait."

———•·•———

"I remembered the beer, forgot my fishing rod."

"They moved the lake and I couldn't find it."

———•◦•———

"The truck ran out of gas
in front of a bar."

———•◦•———

"Fish spend all day in schools!"

———•◦•———

"I forgot the beer."

———•◦•———

"The fish can't see the bait."

———•◦•———

"You have to keep your worms warm."

"I guess somebody else caught them all."

"These fish must have lockjaw."

"I couldn't stop shooting at Jet Skis long enough to concentrate on fishing."

"The fish haven't been reading the same how-to books as I have."

"I was at the back of the boat, so all I got was used water."

"They call it 'fishing,' not 'catching.'"

"I think the moon is in the wrong phase."

———•◦•———

"Today was just a scouting trip.
The real event is next week."

———•◦•———

"I got tired of the fish jumping out of the
water to laugh at me."

———•◦•———

"They must have forgotten to stock the lake."

———•◦•———

"My hip flask is empty."

———•◦•———

"The barometric pressure must be dropping."

"Damned activist fish—I think they
were on a hunger strike."

———•◦•———

"I didn't use low-carb bait."

———•◦•———

"Jenny Craig reservoir was not the best place to fish."

———•◦•———

"The other boats were offering all-you-can-eat bait."

———•◦•———

"I was overcome by vegetarianism during the day."

———•◦•———

"The boat sank."

"A suicide fish on a jihad blew up the boat."

———•—••—•———

"PETA protest."

———•—••—•———

"He kept screaming, 'Swim away, Nemo!'
so we came home."

———•—••—•———

"They were actually checking for licenses today."

———•—••—•———

"They should call this thing a 'repel' instead of a 'lure.'"

———•—••—•———

"We used Brie instead of Velveeta."

Unnecessary Sweating

"It hasn't done a thing for Richard Simmons."

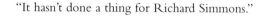

"I would, but my laundry is drying on the treadmill."

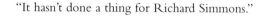

"I'm afraid it will get blood in my alcohol stream."

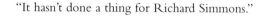

"I only have so many heartbeats left, and I don't want to waste them exercising."

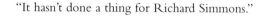

"If I exercise, any time added to my life will have been spent exercising, which means it will have been wasted."

"The elevator at the gym is broken."

———•••———

"I didn't get my Wheaties protein smoothie
this morning."

———•••———

"I want to finish dessert."

———•••———

"My hair will get messed up."

———•••———

"My mom said if I jog, my uterus will fall out."

———•••———

"I'm allergic to sweat."

"I'm trying to cut down on exercise."

———•◦•———

"I don't want to break a nail."

———•◦•———

"My wife would be unhappy with me
if I lost weight."

———•◦•———

"I'm stuck in the doorway."

———•◦•———

"I am in training—sumo training."

———•◦•———

"I'd lift weights, but they're so heavy!"

"The TV at the gym is always on something
I don't want to watch."

———•—•—•———

"I can't bend over to tie my running shoes."

———•—•—•———

"What do you mean, the Macarena's not exercise?"

———•—•—•———

"They won't let me smoke in the gym."

———•—•—•———

"I'm not as fat as those people in the mall."

———•—•—•———

"My leotard shrank."

"I might not have enough energy left over for sex."

"I am in shape. I'm shaped like a pear."

"In Latin, 'exercise' means 'to put out,'
and I'm not that kind of girl."

"My beer goes flat while I'm running."

"I'm really afraid it will become a habit."

"Exercise is just for people who are in shape."

Hygiene, Health, and Style

"I'm afraid I'll shrink in a hot shower."

I guess there are those among us for whom cleanliness is next to impossible. It is, however, so hard just to say, "I'm a pig." That comes across as such a personal failing in today's society. So the well-prepared slob knows just what to say when that moment arrives and a friend or acquaintance appears to be fighting nausea. And what of health concerns? Well, most people would rather not bathe for a month than visit a doctor or dentist.

Personal and Domicile Failures

"I have a part in a show about coal miners."

———•◆•———

"I think I look good in dirt."

———•◆•———

"Washing off the natural oils is really bad for your skin."

"Pigpen was always my favorite Peanuts character."

———•◆•———

"After seeing *Jaws*, I can't get in water of any kind."

———•◆•———

"The batteries in the mop are dead."

———•◆•———

"I have a rash that keeps me from shaving."

———•◆•———

"I'm creating a protective layer of dirt so
I don't get skin cancer."

———•◆•———

"Don't you know deodorant gives you cancer?"

"Millions of Frenchmen can't be wrong!"

———•◦•———

"My clothes are a biological experiment
on bacteria growth."

———•◦•———

"Clothing gremlins threw my clothes on
the floor and stomped on them."

———•◦•———

"I was going for the 1970s PGA tour look."

———•◦•———

"I needed a comb and all I could find was a spatula."

———•◦•———

"Fraternity hazing."

"Men don't have to shave their legs."

———•◦•———

"Tomorrow is laundry day."

———•◦•———

"There are so many brands of soap,
I can't decide which one to use."

———•◦•———

"Water makes me break out in a rash."

———•◦•———

"A man's home is his smelly,
disgusting, repugnant castle!"

———•◦•———

"I haven't cleaned up from the rhino stampede."

"Soon it will be the world's
first indoor landfill."

———•◆•———

"The cleaning lady died."

———•◆•———

"Disorder is a sign of creative ability."

———•◆•———

"The dishwasher broke. I don't know how
to do dishes by hand."

———•◆•———

"Einstein had a messy desk."

———•◆•———

"I want my husband to leave me."

"They're stuck to the floor."

———•◦•———

"Think of an anal retentive personality,
and then think of the exact opposite."

———•◦•———

"I cleaned it up last year. I'm not in a hurry
to repeat that experience."

———•◦•———

"I don't like that detergent—it leaves a film."

———•◦•———

"Vandals broke in while we were out."

"Some friends we don't really like are coming over later."

———•◦•———

"I had a really harrowing vacuum-cleaner
experience as a child."

———•◦•———

"Last time I cleaned the place up, I couldn't
find anything for a month."

———•◦•———

"It's a union job. I don't have a card."

———•◦•———

"With this back, I can't lift
anything heavier than a beer."

Domestic Duties on Crack

For those times when you need an excuse and all you have is the house, don't say something legitimately true. Go with the bizarre—it's much more fun.

> "All this whale blubber has really plugged up the kitchen sink."

> "My son found out you can't flush a squash down the toilet even if you beat it with a hammer."

> "I was drilling for oil in the living room and hit a gusher."

> "Joe tried to fix the plumbing—there's no hot water and the sink dispenses natural gas."

"That pudding piñata we bought for my kid's
birthday made a real mess."

———•◦•———

"The neighbor's cannon went off and blew
a hole in the garage."

———•◦•———

"The main beer line coming into the house is leaking."

———•◦•———

"We're replacing the cauldron and open fire with a
modern water heater."

———•◦•———

"The guy is here to fumigate for cobras."

"The foundation has lost confidence and the
house is starting to lean."

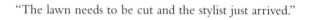

"Not now—I've got raw lard pouring into the basement."

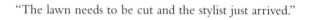

"The lawn needs to be cut and the stylist just arrived."

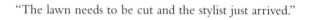

"I have to fix the food disposal—it burps after each use."

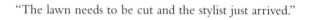

"The toilet is lobbying for improved working conditions."

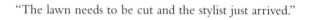

"We're replacing the water heater with a light
water nuclear reactor."

"We have a chipmunk infestation."

———•—•———

"Saturday we're painting the carpet a different color."

———•—•———

"I'm tearing out all the ceilings to
create more headroom."

———•—•———

"I'm up to my knees in knee-high stuff."

———•—•———

"A pack of rapid beavers destroyed the back fence."

———•—•———

"The electric fence around the house is on the fritz."

"We have genius termites—they carved
'GET OUT' in the wall."

———•—•—•———

"We're installing a one-way window in
our kids' bedroom."

———•—•—•———

"I'm building a guest house for the dog's visitors."

———•—•—•———

"Since the state doubled our property taxes, we're
tearing down half the house."

———•—•—•———

"I have to get ten pounds of herring out of the toilet."

I Feel Fine, Really

Avoiding Doctors

"Every time I go, he finds something
wrong with me. I'm not going back!"

———•·•———

"He won't let me play with those shock-paddle thingies."

———•·•———

"All he keeps in the waiting area are copies of
Morticians Quarterly."

———•·•———

"Last time I went in for a cold, she insisted on
checking my prostate."

———•·•———

"I'm afraid he'll take one look at my pupils
and realize the truth."

"When he says he's in practice, he means it literally."

———•◦•———

"Those paper robes are really drafty."

———•◦•———

"I can't see anyone again who uses the phrase 'stool sample.'"

———•◦•———

"I'm paranoid I won't be able to fill that cup."

———•◦•———

"We're not supposed to see each other until after the trial."

———•◦•———

"I went in for an appendectomy and came out without a kidney."

"She is so biased against people who smoke and drink."

———•—•———

"But nothing hurts at the moment."

———•—•———

"If he cares so much, why doesn't he come and see me?"

———•—•———

"I'm starting to enjoy the part where
she asks me to cough."

———•—•———

"I don't like to be touched there unless I get a kiss first."

———•—•———

"I found out he went to school at the
University of Guadalajara."

"I'm sure it's just gas . . . and a little internal bleeding."

———•+•+———

"I saw my doctor last week on *60 Minutes*."

———•+•+———

"I dated his nurse for a while."

———•+•+———

"That place is just packed with sick people!"

———•+•+———

"The doctor's office isn't on the way to the bar."

———•+•+———

"I'm afraid she'll realize I have gills."

———•+•+———

"The gestation period isn't over yet."

Avoiding Dentists

"I'm trying to be the youngest person
ever to get dentures."

———•◦•———

"I just don't think laughing gas is all that funny."

———•◦•———

"That guy hires the ugliest dental assistants."

———•◦•———

"I can work on my own teeth just fine, thank you."

———•◦•———

"I don't want anyone putting their hands in my mouth."

———•◦•———

"I've got more teeth than I need anyway."

"My dentist still doesn't use modern techniques—
it's like a torture chamber."

———•◦•———

"My teeth are pretty crowded as it is."

———•◦•———

"They always play the worst music while
he works on my teeth."

———•◦•———

"I really like soup."

———•◦•———

"I'm going for the Appalachian look."

———•◦•———

"Didn't you hear about those people who contracted
AIDS from their dentists?"

"George Washington had wooden teeth,
and he did just fine."

———•◆•———

"That's what the toothpaste is for."

———•◆•———

"I can't let him find the radio transmitter."

———•◆•———

Keeping Up Appearances (or Not)

"I want to reassure you that I am not this size, really. Dear
me, no, I am being amplified by the mike."

—*G. K. Chesterton, portly British essayist, novelist, and poet,*
giving a lecture in Pittsburgh

———•◆•———

"My clients are in the counterculture.
We have to connect."

"I work undercover."

———•—•———

"Clothing burglars stole every fashionable thing I had!"

———•—•———

"The cleaner shrunk my clothes."

———•—•———

"There is no excuse for my appearance,
but there are many reasons."

—*Phyllis Diller*

———•—•———

"I'm color-blind."

———•—•———

"The power's out in my bedroom."

"Isn't today Halloween?"

———•·•———

"I'm not bad. I'm just drawn that way."

—*Jessica Rabbit, in the film*
Who Framed Roger Rabbit?

———•·•———

"All my taste is in my mouth."

———•·•———

"I'm seeing a counselor for fashion-victim therapy."

———•·•———

"Applying makeup in a moving car has its complications."

———•·•———

"Somebody told me the Tammy Faye look is back."

419

"My barber is very old and nearly blind."

———•◦•———

"How can you even ask me? Dear Kitchener saw
me in that hat twice!"

—*Lady Margot Asquith, British writer and socialite,
when asked by her stepdaughter if she planned to
wear a particular hat to Lord Kitchener's
memorial service*

———•◦•———

"Hormonal therapy run amuck."

———•◦•———

"The fashion police were occupied at the donut shop."

———•◦•———

"I'm protesting the rigid conformity of a fascist society!"

"I'm a huge Lakers fan—I always wear the colors."

"I saw a Cosmo article on the resurgence
of Amish hairstyles."

"I'm having a bad back-hair day."

"I'm part of a social science experiment on
repelling the opposite sex."

"It's genetic. My parents dressed like crap, too."

"I've been making all my own clothes."

"Naugahyde is useful for more than just furniture."

———•·•———

"Why are women the only ones
who get to wear skirts?"

———•·•———

"I'm honoring my ancestors—African pygmy warriors."

———•·•———

"I'm fascinated with clowns."

———•·•———

"Flock of Seagulls fetish."

———•·•———

"Cryogenics. I just thawed out after twenty-five years."

"My wife took up knitting."

———•◦•———

"I thought, 'That old carpet would make a
great winter sweater.'"

———•◦•———

"Too many beatings with the ugly stick."

———•◦•———

"My research has paid off: there is such a thing
as too much Botox."

———•◦•———

"I found out too late my plastic surgeon has
a drinking problem."

———•◦•———

"I only have funhouse mirrors in my apartment."

"My grandmother loves to see me in last
year's Christmas gifts."

A Nibble on the Nails

"I think my fingers could be shorter."

"I'm on that Atkins protein diet."

"I save money on nail clippers and corn chips."

"I'm really into organic food."

"I can't reach my toenails."

"I like to always have snacks on hand."

———•—•———

"They won't let me work with sharp objects."

———•—•———

Just a Nip and a Tuck

"Getting bigger breasts is really a career decision."

———•—•———

"I'm tired of my chin falling into my plate."

———•—•———

"I told him I'm only forty."

———•—•———

"So I can be ready for my closeup, Mr. DeMille."

"I just can't try and jog it off anymore."

———•◦•———

"I want to donate extra skin to burn victims."

———•◦•———

"I'd much rather live my life as Cher."

———•◦•———

"My nose is so big, flowers cower in fear."

———•◦•———

"I want to look more like you."

———•◦•———

"I want to use the excess to build another me."

"Looking old is just so passé these days."

———•◦•———

"I'm thinking of a career move to the porn industry."

———•◦•———

"I always want to be able to float if I fall out of a boat."

———•◦•———

"My brother-in-law just finished med
school and needs the practice."

———•◦•———

"I can't keep shaving this many chins."

———•◦•———

"I want to have webbed hands and feet."

"I want to get reacquainted with my feet."

———•—•—•———

"I can't stand any more birds landing on my nose."

———•—•—•———

"This third ear just isn't doing anything for me."

———•—•—•———

"My son's friend asked how long he'd been living with grandma."

———•—•—•———

"Nobody whistles when I walk by construction sites."

———•—•—•———

"Size matters."

Addiction and Indulgences

"I tossed a coin and unadulterated reality lost."

Aren't sin taxes enough punishment for alcohol and tobacco consumption? Apparently not, because many of us still feel we need an excuse.

Libations

"Dinner without wine is like a bald woman."

———•◆•———

"Isn't there a water shortage?"

———•◆•———

"If God wanted us to abstain, he wouldn't have created fermentation."

———•◆•———

"I only drink to steady my nerves. Sometimes I'm so steady I don't move for months."

—*W. C. Fields*

"I'm much cuter and sexier after a few rounds."

———•·•———

"Bubejikelsingugothom."

———•·•———

"I'm having dinner with my parents later."

———•·•———

"Booze is like jet fuel, and I'm a rocket ready
to blast off, baby!"

———•·•———

"I'm not all that keen on remembering
where I've been."

———•·•———

"I like to have an excuse for making an ass of myself."

"All I know is, I woke up and I am covered in cream."

—*Peter Buck, of the band REM, explaining what he remembered about a supposed charge against him of "air rage" in which he blacked out and overturned a breakfast cart on an airplane. Buck blamed the incident on a sleeping pill combined with a drink and was acquitted.*

"Why carry around all these extra unused brain cells?"

"There was no warning label."

"I'm equipped with a bionic liver."

"I'm terribly allergic to not having beer regularly."

"The bartender is the best therapist I've ever had."

———•◆•———

"Sobriety was just such a disappointment."

———•◆•———

"I really only come here to play darts."

———•◆•———

"It makes me less astute and you more attractive."

———•◆•———

On Drugs

"I was under medication when I made the
decision not to burn the tapes."

—*President Richard Nixon*

" ... and I didn't like it. I didn't inhale it
and I never tried it again."

—*President Bill Clinton, speaking freely of his
experimentation with marijuana during college days*

"Crack is cheap. I make too much money
to use crack. Crack is wack."

—*Whitney Houston, on why crack was not included
in a lengthy listing of drugs she used*

The Noxious Weed

"On my planet, cigarette smoke is like oxygen is here."

"I just hate that 'fresh, clean laundry' smell."

"The only sure way to quit is the Swedish method,
and I can't afford the airfare."

———•—•———

"Young lady, I am not smoking this cigar.
I am transporting it to the next floor."

—*Congressman Jack Brady, when reproached by a young
woman for smoking in an elevator*

———•—•———

"My body turns the smoke into fuel."

———•—•———

"I had a lot of complaints about my
blindingly white teeth."

———•—•———

"My doctor told me I was overly healthy."

"I just had my lungs hosed out last weekend."

———•◆•———

"My hands would die of boredom."

———•◆•———

"I'm just trying to displace the pollution
with something cleaner."

———•◆•———

"It's faster than waiting for secondhand smoke to work."

———•◆•———

"I really want to lower my voice an octave."

———•◆•———

"It's my long-term plan for changing
the color of my apartment."

"I didn't want the cigarette lighter to feel unwanted."

"I use clouds of smoke to hide my escape route."

"I can't help but put burning things in my mouth."

Buying, Buying, and . . . Well, Buying

"I want to have better clothes to give to charity."

"I understand BMWs really retain their value."

"I'm just trying to be a good American citizen."

"I've earned these shoes."

"We've got to pause and ask ourselves:
How much clean air do we need?"

—*Lee Iacocca, of Ford Motor Company, on the 1974
opposition among Detroit automakers to tougher
automobile emission standards*

"I'm feeling a little anemic—I need a plasma TV."

"I saved so much on the pants, I should
buy some new shoes."

"I'm barefoot."

"I should celebrate with some new shoes."

———•—•———

"I'll save even more if I buy seven."

———•—•———

"We need authorization. As an oil company
we can't just go out and start [cleaning up]."

—*Lawrence Rawl, official spokesperson for Exxon Corporation,
explaining why in 1989 the company waited two days before
trying to clean the mess from the Valdez oil spill in Alaska*

———•—•———

"It's okay—I stole this credit card."

———•—•———

"Well, I'm not leaving all that money to my kids!"

"That was a very convincing sales pitch."

———•◆•———

"My counselor calls this plastic therapy."

———•◆•———

"I'm only trying to support those poor
people in Honduras."

———•◆•———

"This is the equivalent of sex for me."

———•◆•———

"It's better than using heroin!"

———•◆•———

"If I don't shop I'll start to shake and break out in sweats."

"It's my opportunity to give change to the homeless people by the mall."

———•••———

"He won't call me if I don't buy anything."

———•••———

"The TV ad said I could not miss this sale."

———•••———

"Their advertising really moved me."

———•••———

"The spokesman reminds me of my grandfather."

———•••———

"I'm so susceptible to subliminal messages."

"I'm trying to work past
my shopaphobia."

———•—•—

"This bizarre skin ailment means
I can only wear silk."

———•—•—

"I'm an absolute believer in
homo economicus."

———•—•—

"I must stay true to the time-honored
traditions of my people."

———•—•—

"Because I really, really want it."

Transportation

"But if I get a new car, I won't have this one as an excuse!"

The ever-popular traffic jam isn't the only excuse you can draw from the world of transportation. Try a more creative transportation excuse the next time you fail to show up or fulfill your obligations.

The Horseless Carriage

"My car got stuck in a tar pit."

"I locked myself in my car."

"The keys to my car were seized as evidence."

"We got four flat tires at once."

"I was taking the shortcut through the canyon when a huge rock came screaming down the hill and ripped through my windshield, missing my head and landing in the backseat. I was wearing a skirt, of course, because you want me to, and my legs got a few cuts from the glass, so I went to the hospital to get cleaned up. My car isn't drivable anymore, so I had to get a ride from my brother. So, that's why I'm wearing pants . . . and I'm late."

———•◆•———

"I drive a British sports car."

———•◆•———

"I'm protesting the price of gas by refusing to buy any."

———•◆•———

"I listened to those guys on Car Talk."

———•◆•———

"I had to wait until my car was fully charged."

"My girlfriend broke up with me in that car—
I decided today I can never drive it again."

⎯⎯•◦•⎯⎯

"The energy crisis has left me too weak to drive."

⎯⎯•◦•⎯⎯

"I found out today my car is not amphibious."

⎯⎯•◦•⎯⎯

"I got pulled over for an episode of *COPS*."

⎯⎯•◦•⎯⎯

"I can't find the starter crank for my car."

⎯⎯•◦•⎯⎯

"I couldn't find a parking space
my Hummer would fit into."

"Somebody stole the engine out of my car."

———•———

"I got pulled over for not wearing pants."

———•———

"I picked up a hitchhiker and he forced
me to drive him to Mexico."

———•———

"I bought a Dodge Stealth and now I can't find it."

———•———

"I took apart the engine over the weekend
to see how it works."

———•———

"I can't risk driving on the highway without doors."

"I didn't name the car Christine for no reason."

———•◦•———

"The cops pulled me over for speeding and found a body in the trunk."

———•◦•———

"I started to yield and just couldn't stop."

———•◦•———

"The sign said stop, but it never said go."

———•◦•———

"My front tires disagreed about the best way to get here."

———•◦•———

"I had to pull over and watch for slow children."

"I ran over a banana peel and slid into a tree."

———•◦•———

"A strange voice on the radio told me to pull over and wait for further instructions."

———•◦•———

"It took me longer than usual to lose the cops."

———•◦•———

Getting from A to B

"The train hit a water buffalo this morning. What a mess!"

———•◦•———

"Somebody put a lock on the door of the freight car."

———•◦•———

"The cab driver didn't speak English."

"Hitchhiking just isn't as successful as it used to be."

"My dogsled broke down, and I didn't have a spare dog."

"It takes time to inflate a dirigible every morning."

"My tuk-tuk driver insisted
on taking me to the reclining Buddha."

"The front tire of my motorcycle got stuck
in the train tracks."

"My horse threw a shoe and a wheel
came off the buggy."

"A strong downdraft drove my hang glider
into the ground."

"The ferry hit an iceberg."

"Very stubborn mules."

"The subway mistakenly ventured
below the water table."

"The train ran out of coal."

"I fell asleep on the train and woke
up in Poughkeepsie."

"The streetcar had a flat tire . . . it ran out of gas."

———•••———

"They wouldn't let me on the bus without pants."

———•••———

"It took me a while to hail a limousine."

———•••———

"I was paddling upstream."

———•••———

"Arab terrorists forced us to fly to Syria."

———•••———

"The camels refused to cooperate."

———•••———

"My unicycle was impounded and I had to walk."

History

"I could have invented the wheel, but I was raised in a disadvantaged clan."

How has the excuse been put to use throughout the history of our species? Whenever the need has arisen, humankind has found a way to deflect blame and stave off humiliation. After exploring the evolution of the excuse, you can draw on history to create your own excuses or you can create history with an illustrious excuse.

A (True) History of Conflict

"He lobbed his nuclear warheads at me first!"

Let's revisit the difference between excuses and reasons or explanations. The bombing of Pearl Harbor wasn't an excuse for entering World War II, it was a factual, verifiable reason. Since 1945, however, our "reasons" for entering war have turned out not to be true.

The Spanish-American War

"Remember the Maine! To hell with Spain!"

—This rallying cry followed the February 15, 1898, explosion aboard the U.S.S. Maine in Havana; the explosion, resulting from a coal fuel accident, gave those who wanted war with Spain ample ammunition, while Spain sought to avoid the conflict.

World War II

"Well, sir, this paper has a policy not to publish any ads."

—*Dashiell Hammett, novelist, when asked while working as an editor during World War II why he gave a great deal of coverage to Russian activity but very little to the Americans*

———•◦•———

The Cold War

"I was a pilot flying an airplane and it just so happened that where I was flying made what I was doing spying."

—*Francis Gary Powers, U2 pilot shot down over the Soviet Union in 1960 and held for spying*

———•◦•———

The Vietnam War

"I announced to the American people that the North Vietnamese regime . . . conducted . . . deliberate attacks against U.S. naval vessels operating in international waters."

—*President Lyndon B. Johnson, speaking to Congress on August 5, 1964. In 1995, former Secretary of Defense Robert McNamara said the Gulf of Tonkin torpedo attack referred to here never occurred.*

"It was necessary to destroy the village to save it."

—*American officer, quoted in a 1968 report on the obliteration of the Vietnamese village of Ben Tre*

———•◦•———

Iran-Contra Scandal

"Mistakes were made."

—*President Ronald Reagan, on the Iran-Contra scandal. Making use of an alternative to the excuse, the obfuscation of blame, Reagan delivers an admission that does not suggest who might have made the mistakes.*

———•◦•———

The Persian Gulf War, 1990–1991

"I saw the Iraqi soldiers come into the hospital with guns and go into the room where . . . babies were in incubators. They took the babies out of the incubators, took the incubators, and left the babies on the cold floor to die."

—*Nayirah, a fifteen-year-old Kuwaiti girl, testifying before Congress on October 10, 1990. This emotionally wrenching tale contributed to the buildup toward the Gulf War. A complete fabrication, Nayirah's testimony failed to reveal she was the daughter of the Kuwaiti ambassador to the United States.*

That War in Iraq 2003–?

The search for weapons of mass destruction, cited as the reason for the return to Iraq, is an incredibly rich source for excuse-makers, should you ever need to engage in a large-scale conflict. Not all of the statements listed here are excuses; some statements are intended simply to support excuses made by the administration. Taken collectively, they embody quite an excuse.

"[Saddam Hussein] has not developed any significant capability with respect to weapons of mass destruction. He is unable to project conventional power against his neighbors."

—*Secretary of State Colin Powell, speaking in Cairo, Egypt, on February 24, 2001*

"[Saddam Hussein] has weapons of mass destruction. The lesser risk is in preemption. We've got to stop wishing away the problem."

—*Defense Policy Board Chairman Richard Perle, November 2001*

"Simply stated, there is no doubt that Saddam Hussein now has weapons of mass destruction. There is no doubt that he is amassing them to use against our friends, against our allies, and against us."

—*Vice President Dick Cheney, August 26, 2002*

———•◆•———

"There are a number of terrorist states pursuing weapons of mass destruction—Iran, Libya, North Korea, Syria, just to name a few—but no terrorist state poses a greater or more immediate threat to the security of our people than the regime of Saddam Hussein and Iraq."

—*Secretary of Defense Donald Rumsfeld, September 19, 2002*

———•◆•———

"Our conservative estimate is that Iraq today has a stockpile of between one hundred and five hundred tons of chemical weapons agent. That is enough agent to fill sixteen thousand battlefield rockets."

—*Colin Powell, February 5, 2003*

"Let's talk about the nuclear proposition for a minute. We know that based on intelligence, that he has been very, very good at hiding these kinds of efforts. He's had years to get good at it, and we know he has been absolutely devoted to trying to acquire nuclear weapons. And we believe he has, in fact, reconstituted nuclear weapons."

—*Dick Cheney, March 16, 2003*

———•◦•———

"I have no doubt that we're going to find big stores of weapons of mass destruction."

—*Kenneth Adelman, member of the Pentagon's Defense Policy Board and signatory to the Project for the New American Century, March 23, 2003*

———•◦•———

"We have high confidence that they have weapons of mass destruction. That is what this war was about and it is about. And we have high confidence it will be found."

—*White House Press Secretary Ari Fleischer, April 10, 2003*

"We never believed that we'd just tumble over weapons of mass destruction in that country. We're going to find what we find as a result of talking to people, I believe, not simply by going to some site and hoping to discover it."

—*Donald Rumsfeld, May 4, 2004, three days after the administration declared the end of major combat operations*

"I'm not surprised if we begin to uncover the weapons program of Saddam Hussein—because he had a weapons program."

—*President George W. Bush, May 6, 2003*

"Now, what happened? Why weren't [the WMDs] used? I don't know. There are several possible reasons for that . . . it may very well be that they didn't have time to . . . use chemical weapons. It is also possible that they decided that they would destroy them prior to a conflict."

—*Donald Rumsfeld, May 27, 2003*

"For bureaucratic reasons, we settled on one issue—weapons of mass destruction—because it was the one reason everyone could agree on."

—*Deputy Secretary of Defense Paul Wolfowitz, May 28, 2003*

"It was a surprise to me then, it remains a surprise to me now, that we have not uncovered weapons . . . in some of the forward dispersal sites. Again, believe me, it's not for lack of trying. We've been to virtually every ammunition supply point between the Kuwaiti border and Baghdad, but they're simply not there. We were simply wrong."

—*Lieutenant General James T. Conway, U.S. Marine Corps, speaking at a press conference, May 30, 2003*

"I don't know anybody that I can think of who has contended that the Iraqis had nuclear weapons."

—*Donald Rumsfeld, June 24, 2003*

"I'm not sure that's the major reason we went to war."

—*Senator Majority Leader Bill Frist, Republican from Tennessee, speaking in regard to weapons of mass destruction, June 26, 2003*

————◆————

"Saddam Hussein had biological and chemical weapons that were unaccounted for that we're still confident we'll find. I think the burden is on those people who think he didn't have weapons of mass destruction to tell the world where they are . . .just because they haven't yet been found doesn't mean they didn't exist. The burden is on the critics to explain where the weapons of mass destruction are. If they think they were destroyed, the burden is on them to explain when he destroyed them and where he destroyed them."

—*Ari Fleischer, July 9, 2003*

————◆————

"I said, 'We know they're in that area.' I should have said, 'I believe they're in that area.' Our intelligence tells us they're in that area, and that was our best judgment."

—*Donald Rumsfeld, September 10, 2003*

"I don't think they existed. I think there were stockpiles at the end of the first Gulf War and those were . . . a combination of U.N. inspectors and unilateral Iraqi action got rid of them. I think the best evidence is that they did not resume large-scale production, and that's what we're really talking about, is large stockpiles, not the small. Large stockpiles of chemical and biological weapons in the period after '95."

—Dr. David Kay, appointed by the Central Intelligence Agency to lead the Iraq Survey Group in investigating whether or not weapons of mass destruction existed in Iraq, speaking on January 23, 2004

"When I made that presentation in February 2003, it was based on the best information that the Central Intelligence Agency made available to me. We studied it carefully; we looked at the sourcing in the case of the mobile trucks and trains. There was multiple sourcing for that. Unfortunately, that multiple sourcing over time has turned out to be not accurate. And so I'm deeply disappointed . . . it turned out that the sourcing was inaccurate and wrong and, in some cases, deliberately misleading. And for that, I am disappointed and I regret it."

—Colin Powell, May 16, 2004

"I always said that Saddam Hussein was a threat. He was a threat because he had used weapons of mass destruction against his own people. He was a threat because he was a sworn enemy to the United States of America, just like al Qaeda. He was a threat because he had terrorist connections—not only al Qaeda connections, but other connections to terrorist organizations; Abu Nidal was one. He was a threat because he provided safe-haven for a terrorist like Zarqawi, who is still killing innocents inside of Iraq. No, he was a threat, and the world is better off and America is more secure without Saddam Hussein in power."

—*President George W. Bush, June 17, 2004.*

Top Ten Excuses for Not Finding Weapons of Mass Destruction

Enjoy this thoughtful summary of excuses, courtesy of the writers at *Late Night with David Letterman*.

10. "We've only looked through ninety-nine percent of the country."

9. "We spent entire budget making those playing cards."

8. "Containers are labeled in some crazy language."

7. "They must have been stolen by some of them evil X-Men mutants."

6. "Did I say Iraq has weapons of mass destruction? I meant they have goats."

5. "How are we supposed to find weapons of mass destruction when we can't even find Cheney?"

4. "Still screwed because of Daylight Saving Time."

3. "When you're trying to find something, it's always in the last place you look—am I right, people?"

2. "Let's face it—I ain't exactly a genius."

1. "Geraldo took them!"

Underutilized Excuses, by Region or Era

Ancient Egypt

"Cleopatra's a real stunner, but Mark Anthony would kick
my ass if I even said hello."

———•◦•———

"No more statues of Ramses until he pays me
for the last one."

———•◦•———

"Lift another stone onto this damned pyramid?
Look at the blister I have already!"

———•◦•———

Ancient Greece

"Socrates is dead? Oh, what a time to
get my toga refitted."

"I'm sure they just left a huge wooden
horse as parting gift."

———•◆•———

"I would love to go conquering with Alexander,
but this arthritis . . ."

———•◆•———

"Aristotle is just too New Age for me. I'll stick with my
Tales from Olympus comics."

———•◆•———

The Time of Christ

"He wants to go see the lepers? Umm . . . I've got to
work at Starbucks in ten minutes."

———•◆•———

"That Pilate gives me the creeps.
I'm going to skip the meeting."

"Sorry I missed the crucifixion. I couldn't
find chariot parking."

Ancient Rome

"Oh, forget about it. I can't tell which one is Spartacus."

"I bet on the Christians every time we go,
and I have yet to win anything!"

"All that Caesar ever does is talk about himself.
Let's just stay home and order in Greek food."

Spanish Inquisition

"Oh, heretic! No, I'm not one of those.
I thought you said something else."

"I would set her on fire, but we're fresh out of matches."

———•••———

Middle Ages

"When you said you wanted the Holy Grail,
I didn't think you meant today."

———•••———

"I can't go on another crusade until
I get my luggage back from the last one."

———•••———

"I know you said you wanted a round table,
but this one was on sale."

———•••———

The Renaissance

"I'd love to help out, but I have this painting to finish, a
block of marble to carve, poetry to compose . . . "

World War II

"He just has a thing about Poland."

Underutilized Excuses, for Historical Figures

"I learned pig Latin instead of the regular stuff.
The other kids made fun of me."

—*Julius Caesar*

"I can't help it. I was born terrible."

—*Ivan the Terrible*

"There weren't many positive role models
in my community."

—*Attila the Hun*

"Violent computer games, I would imagine.
And too much AC/DC . . . "

—*Genghis Khan*

"I thought everybody liked cake. I like cake.
Don't you like cake?"

—*Marie Antoinette*

"It's these damned winters. They make me crazy."

—*Josef Stalin*

"I figured, what the hell . . . I've got two."

—*Vincent Van Gogh*

"Really, I'm just a frustrated artist
trying to express himself."

—*Adolf Hitler*

"Because I could."

—*Bill Clinton*

"Because he could."

—*Monica Lewinsky*

"If you had to go through life with this name,
how would you handle it?"

—*Pol Pot*

"You know, I was hungry, the fridge was empty . . .
you do the math."

—*Jeffrey Dahmer*

"I trace it all back to a fraternity hazing incident involving strawberry Jell-O and all-beef hot dogs. Things haven't been the same since."

—*Richard Nixon*

"There were the WBGs, and we had to attacknify what was . . . you know, them're better off now, those Iraqians, there's freedom, and New Coke and stuff."

—*President George W. Bush*

"I would more accurately portray my recent statement as a clarification instead of a reversal. I rarely flip, and I have never flopped."

—*John Kerry*

Politics

"No reasonable person would consider this a payoff!"

Who is really at fault? In politics, no one is ever personally responsible. The cast of culprits is lengthy, time-tested, and utilized by all who occupy elected office. The better question is, who would you like to fault?

> "As an excuse that is not enough, but as an explanation it is ample."

—*Italian aristocrat, after being jostled on a train platform in Rome by Hermann Goering, second in command in Hitler's Third Reich, and demanding an apology for the offense; Goering responded to the demand with, "I am Hermann Goering."*

I think when [Bill Clinton] was governor and not paying proper taxes, he was trying to find sources of income to please [Hillary]. He seeks money for the woman's pleasure, to buy her gifts. Women push men to crime."

—*Vladimir Zhirinovsky, Russian politician.*

"Well, they're multipurpose pliers.
Not only do they put the clips on, but they take them off."

—*Spokesperson for Pratt and Whitney, defense contractor,
on why the company charged the Pentagon $999 each for
ordinary pliers.*

"I didn't accept it. I received it."

—*Richard Allen, national security advisor to President Ronald
Reagan, trying to explain gifts he "received" in exchange for
arranging an interview with the first lady.*

"They gave you a book of checks. They didn't
ask for any deposits."

—*U.S. Representative Joe Early of Massachusetts,
on the House banking scandal.*

"If I tell a lie it's only because I think
I'm telling the truth."

—*Phil Gaglardi, minister of highways for British Columbia.*

"I accept honoraria. I do not like to do it . . . . We do have grandchildren to educate. . . . If it were not for their grandparents, one of these grandsons would not be graduating as a physics major this year. Another grandchild would not be entering as a freshman to college this year. It is important that this country graduate physics majors, majors in mathematics, chemistry, and various other disciplines in order to keep this country ahead in technology, science, and physics."

—*U.S. Senator Robert Byrd of West Virginia, explaining why he finds it necessary to accept something he finds unpalatable*

———————

"It's not like molesting young girls or young boys. It's not a showstopper."

—*U.S. Representative Charlie Wilson of Texas, on the revelation in 1992 that he had bounced eighty-one checks at the House of Representatives' bank, including one to the IRS.*

———————

"I was not lying. I said things that later on seemed to be untrue."

—*Richard Nixon, looking back on Watergate in 1978.*

"I may have said something about the NAACP being un-American or communist, but I meant no harm by it."

—*Jefferson B. Sessions III, unsuccessful federal court nominee.*

"I have not reneged on a promise.
I have changed my mind."

—*Pierre Rinfret, candidate for governor of New York,
on why he did not make public all of his tax returns.*

"It was suggested I have this picture taken with Miss Rice. This attractive lady whom I had only recently been introduced to dropped into my lap. I was embarrassed. I chose not to dump her off and the picture was taken."

—*Gary Hart, 1988 Democratic presidential candidate, on
how photos of him with a young blond woman on his lap
happened to be taken after he was accused of infidelity and
then challenged the press to follow him.*

"She wore her name tags right over her boobs .... I don't think it was right for her to have her name tag on in a—it should be up high. She's not exactly heavily stacked, okay? So I told her ... to move the darn name tag off her boobs."

—*U.S. Representative Ernest Konnyu of California, attempting to explain why he said to a female aide, "Why you got your boob covered up?"*

———•—•—•———

"I wanted to do it, but my children wouldn't let me."

—*Silvio Berlusconi, Italian prime minister and head of a media empire, on why he did not divest of his media interests to avoid conflict-of-interest charges upon taking office.*

———•—•—•———

"No, no, that's just my friends making excuses for me."

—*Robert F. Kennedy, President John F. Kennedy's brother and attorney general, on the suggestion that he was considered ruthless because he had been required to do all the dirty work in his brother's 1960 presidential campaign.*

"First, it was not a strip bar, it was an erotic club. And second, what can I say? I'm a night owl."

—*Marion Barry, former mayor of Washington, D.C.*

———•◦•———

"Oh, that was just an accident that happened."

—*Richard Nixon, offering in 1973 an explanation for how one of the Watergate tapes mysteriously had eighteen minutes erased from it.*

———•◦•———

"Far from being a Congressional junket, this trip will take us to areas which I believe we need to visit to understand the dimensions of the problems confronting U.S. national security and to meet the responsibilities we face as members of the subcommittee on defense."

—*U.S. Senator Daniel Inouye of Hawaii, describing a 1989 trip to Europe and the Mediterranean, with visits to museums, art galleries, and historical sites; wives of staff were included on the trip to deal with "certain responsibilities of protocol."*

"We didn't have the address."

—*Secretary of Defense Caspar Weinberger, under President Ronald Reagan, on why the U.S. had invited Australia but not New Zealand to participate in the development of a strategic defense system.*

"Everybody kept their shoes there. The maids . . . everybody."

—*Imelda Marcos, former first lady of the Philippines, trying in 1986 to explain the more than three thousand pairs of shoes she kept in the presidential palace.*

"His sense of direction was always so bad. There was a family joke about his never knowing what turn to take."

—*Family friend of Senator Edward Kennedy, trying to explain how Kennedy drove off a Massachusetts bridge at Chappaquiddick Island, causing the death of Mary Jo Kopechne.*

Callout: Politicians as Parents

"I'm terribly sorry, but would you mind if my wife and I butted in? The thing is, I've got to go and see the queen at six o'clock."

—British Prime Minister Tony Blair, explaining why he and his wife needed to go ahead of other parents waiting for a parent-teacher conference

———•◦•———

"I wasn't calling as somebody in Washington. I was calling as a mother."

—Lynne Cheney, wife of Vice President Dick Cheney who was then secretary of defense, on a 1989 call to Yellowstone National Park on behalf of her daughter, whose application had been rejected

———•◦•———

"Ronnie was away a lot, you know, and I was alone in that house. . . . It's just a tiny little gun."

—Nancy Reagan, explaining in 1980 why she kept a gun in her nightstand.

"The governments of proper countries are usually on holidays on weekends."

—*Eugene Pozdnayakov, Soviet spokesperson, explaining why the government delayed reporting the 1986 Chernobyl nuclear disaster.*

———•·•———

"I never said I had no idea about most of the things you said I said I had no idea about."

—*Elliott Abrams, Reagan-era assistant secretary of state, in an effort to explain his involvement in the Iran-Contra scandal.*

———•·•———

"This was not a junket in any sense of the word."

—*U.S. Senator Strom Thurmond of South Carolina, explaining a trip in which he, his wife, two children, a next-door neighbor, and eight staff members attended the Paris Air Show at taxpayer expense.*

#1 – It wasn't a fund-raiser, it was a community outreach event.

#2 – No, not a fund-raiser, but something that was finance related.

#3 – Stop saying it was a fund-raiser! It was really a donor-maintenance meeting.

—*Paraphrase of Vice-President Al Gore, attempting valiantly to explain his attendance at a Buddhist temple fund-raiser.*

#1 – "[I was] deliberately excluded . . . unaware . . . denied information."

#2 – "I was out of the loop."

—*President George H. W. Bush, on his involvement in the Iran-Contra scandal.*

"I don't know every damned thing in that ethics law."

—*U.S. Senator Robert Ford of South Carolina, on the fact that he used campaign funds for non-campaign purposes.*

———•◦•———

"I had thought very carefully about committing *hara-kiri* [ritual suicide] over this, but I overslept this morning."

—*Toshio Yamaguchi, former Japanese labor minister, after being arrested and charged with breach of trust related to defunct financial institutions.*

———•◦•———

"He didn't say that. He read what was given to him in a speech."

—*Richard Darman, director of the Office of Management and Budget, on why President George W. Bush failed to keep a campaign pledge.*

"I deliberately fumbled around and didn't do as good as I could. I know that no one remembers what happens in the last two weeks. I gave that guy a false sense of security and he fell for it—hook, line, and sinker."

—*Edward G. Edwards, 1992 candidate for Louisiana governor, on the tactics he used during debate on his opponent.*

———••◦••———

"We may have, because of the things we did, averted World War III. We don't know. And we will never know."

—*U.S. Representative Earl Hilliard of Alabama, identified as the most traveled member of Congress, responding to a question about a month spent in Paris as a member of the committees on agriculture and small business.*

A Final Word

This is going to sound a tad preachy, so I apologize in advance. In compiling this disparate and wacky volume of excuses, particularly those on crime and conflict, it gradually dawned on me that there truly is a dark side to the habit of making excuses. If you've read through most of this book, you will have seen yourself ten times over, as I did, and recognized just how ingrained in our DNA this practice is. I'm not saying that the practice itself is necessarily degrading of society or evil. But there is the slippery slope: Start doing it, and it's hard to stop. In the vernacular of drug addiction, excuse-making is the "gateway" behavior to complete abdication of responsibility.

It isn't hard to look around and find examples of these types of behavior. A serial killer goes to court and his attorney explains, "He wasn't breast fed." A woman parks in the fire lane in front of a grocery store and thinks, "I'll only be here 15 minutes." An elected official fails to meet expectations and says, "It depends on what the meaning of is is." Sure, these examples are not equivalent by any means, but they do all demonstrate a sort of antisocial behavior that says, "I am more important than the expectations of the society that I live in." Taken to a logical end, everyone doing this causes society to dry up and blow away.

The habit of making excuses can rob us of self-esteem, well-being, and success. There are those situations where the only person who believes particular excuses is the one giving them. I recall hearing recently a commentator or analyst say something to the effect of, "Giving up responsibility for ourselves robs us of the core of our being." Certainly, we all know that person who is responsible for nothing, and on whom the sun never shines. In reading through hundreds of excuses, I've been introduced to this dark side of the human psyche in myself. I've enjoyed laughing at many of these excuses as I've read through them, but I've also appreciated seeing that I can follow that laughter down a path that won't benefit me in the long run. I trust that all readers will recognize the same thing for themselves.

But let's not end on a sour note. As is the case with every other scenario or situation in the history of humankind, the truth with regard to making excuses lies somewhere in the middle. In that hallowed central ground between monastic flagellation and criminal irresponsibility lies a balance that always makes allowances for the fair explanation, but never for the unsightly excuse.

Anecdotage. "Excuse Anecdotes." From the Web site: http://www.anecdotage.com/browse.php?term= Excuses

Carroll, Alex. *Speeding Excuses That Work: Escape Tickets Before They Get Written*. Santa Barbara, CA: Gray Area Press, 2004.

Dershowitz, Alan M. *The Abuse Excuse and Other Cop-Outs, Sob Stories, and Evasions of Responsibility*. New York: Little, Brown and Company, 1994.

Ehumor Central. "Real Excuses." From the Web site: http://www.ehumorcentral.com/Directory/Jokes/ 969.html

Hope, Paco. "Excuses for Missing a Day of Work." From the Web site: http://funnies.paco.to/WorkExcuses.html

Myers, Robert A. *Excuses, Excuses: How to Explain Your Way out of Any Situation.* Secaucus, New Jersey: Citadel Press, 1979.

Olive, David. *Political Babble: The 1,000 Dumbest Things Ever Said by Politicians.* New York: Wiley and Sons, 1992.

Parietti, Jeff. *The Greatest Sports Excuses, Alibis, and Explanations.* Chicago: Contemporary Books, 1990.

Petras, Ross and Kathryn. *The Stupidest Things Ever Said by Politicians.* New York: Pocket Books, 1999.

Petras, Ross and Kathryn. *The 776 Stupidest Things Ever Said*. New York: Doubleday, 1993.

Petras, Ross and Kathryn. *The 776 Even Stupider Things Ever Said*. New York: HarperCollins, 1994.

Rotten. "Iraqi WMDs." From the rotten.com Web site: http://www.rotten.com/library/history/war/wmd/saddam

Rutledge, Leigh W. *Excuses, Excuses: A Compendium of Rationalizations, Alibis, Denials, Extenuating Circumstances, and Outright Lies*. New York: Plume, 1992.

Stauber, John, and Sheldon Rampton. "How PR Sold the War in the Persian Gulf." Excerpted from Toxic Sludge is Good for You. From the prwatch.org Web site: http://www.prwatch.org/books/tsigfy10.html

Between periodic displays of piety, David Macfarlane is not averse to the well-used excuse. In fact, the excuse has been a favorite tool of his for some time now:

David came into this world three days late because the traffic was terrible in the birth canal.

He didn't say his first words until three due to some very stuck strained peas.

He didn't walk until five because he couldn't decide whose stride to emulate.

He avoided kissing girls in deference to personal hygiene.

David quit his little-league football team, saying he "never liked the team name."

Though he graduated number 367 in a class of 689, he claimed to have been edged out for valedictorian by "minorities and girls."

David still likes to say Harvard rejected him because he doesn't have the right family name; Idaho State rejected him because he "got the potato question wrong."

David lives in Salt Lake City, Utah, primarily because it is a town where virtually nothing is excusable.

Index

Index

Index

Index

Index

Index

Index

Index